Slipping to Normal

Slipping to Normal

◆

A Matter of Leadership

Bill Arthur

iUniverse, Inc.

New York Lincoln Shanghai

Slipping to Normal
A Matter of Leadership

iUniverse, Inc.

For information address:
iUniverse, Inc.
2021 Pine Lake Road, Suite 100
Lincoln, NE 68512
www.iuniverse.com

ISBN: 0-595-32527-0 (pbk)
ISBN: 0-595-77384-2 (cloth)

Printed in the United States of America

To

Barbara
Steve
Susan, Bob, Will, & Bailey
David, Julie, and Pate

A major portion of time, energy, and thoughts in our family is about the successes and failures of members of the family. It is more than just success or failure in our professions. We are not perfect but we work at it. This book is my way of saying "thanks," and encouraging each of us to keep the faith in each other and in God.

Contents

Acknowledgements

There are many people I must acknowledge and thank. Some have been unwitting contributors throughout my life as we shared ideas, experiences, beliefs, and opinions. I have a lifetime of friends and acquaintances to whom I owe much. Others, more recently, have contributed to this project directly at my request by sharing stories and experiences, and still others have been commentators on the ideas and issues raised in the development of this book. I must acknowledge their contribution and thank them for their enormous help.

My first acknowledgment is that I am not writing as an expert on theology, sociology, philosophy, or anything outside my field of business financial and strategic planning. Neither am I writing as one who has always exemplified the ethical concepts about which I am writing, even though I tried most of the time. I am writing from the experience of one who on occasion has been an unwitting participant in the normalized aggressive self-interests of the "professional management" era, albeit much of the time it was in higher education.

The material in this book is not an expose'. It is simply a book of my own knowledge, experiences, and professional development drawn from readings and from conversations with others in my world. It is my opinion, but it comes from a long professional career. Perhaps sharing these ideas and experiences may help the reader understand how the lack of ethical and moral standards has become a way of life, a normal way of life, systemized by our professional bureaucratized environment. I have written it in hopes that it will get readers thinking and trigger more work and publications by others who are smarter than I am.

There are people who have contributed to my subject over a period of 35 years who did not intend to be quoted so I will not mention their names. Nevertheless, several people contributed directly to the book and I do want to recognize them.

Bill and Sandra Henry read the drafts in detail and made valuable contributions, beyond my expectations. Bill has been a corporate officer in a large publicly traded company throughout a long and successful career. His advice and counsel has been and is deeply appreciated. Sandra has been an executive assistant in a large company and is now Minister of Adult Education at St. Luke UMC, Columbus, Georgia. Dr. Bob McCollum, retired professor of economics at

Columbus State University, helped greatly by resurrecting my tired memory of economics.

Two people have been a great help as editors. Jerry Scott, a good friend, golf buddy, and retired colonel, volunteered to do some editing even when he had his own battle with a physical limitation resulting from surgery for a back injury. Dr. Barbara Hunt, a colleague at Columbus State University and Chair of the Department of Literature and Languages, also made an invaluable contribution as the final editor.

Writing today is much easier than it was when I was a student. It is hard to imagine the tedious work we had to do back in the "good ole days." At least it is easier when the computer does what it is supposed to. When it didn't, I was thankful for Dr. Bob Fleck, Professor on Information Systems at Columbus State University, and Doug Harvey, who built my computer, and John Fugh, who "smartened me up" enough to use it.

Then, there is my family to whom I owe much. When one works at home, it creates a unique set of problems. You are there, but you are not there. You are accessible, but you are not accessible. Their tolerance is greatly appreciated. I hope the result makes it worthwhile.

Preface

I spent more than 35 years in higher education, mostly as department chair and dean of business schools, in one private college but also in three public universities. I, and others of my generation, have also been granted the opportunity to live and work in a period of history when there have been many unique events affecting the way we work, play, relate to one another, and to the way we relate to our Creator. In retrospect, it was fun but at times it was also frustrating. It was a career that I highly recommend to anyone who wants to build something of value for lots of people. If you want to make a contribution to people's lives, to careers, and to your country, the job as dean in a significant university is for you.

The more visible functions of my job were in the usual areas of faculty and student development, and in leading programs of teaching, research, and public service. Each of these responsibilities provided a share of the fun but I also had many opportunities to spend time in conversations with highly intelligent academicians and professionals who contributed to my understanding and interests and to my life's goal of "stamping out ignorance." These conversations made it even more enjoyable, even when we disagreed. Wow! I know some people who will have a heart flutter when they read this.

What was less visible, and unexpected to me in the beginning, were the opportunities for conversations with business leaders who wanted to share their innermost feelings about their own careers and the work they did. On some occasions, they were probably trying to make me feel the importance of what we did in higher education. But the context of the conversations usually was one of concern for what was happening in their world. Frankly, it was a little uncomfortable at times since they were often taking me into their confidence on matters that could harm their careers if the wrong ears heard them. Most often, they would start out, "I always wanted to teach...," or "I would love to have your job." Suspecting a substantial salary differential, my own thoughts were that it might have been terrific to swap jobs with some of them. Instead, in a rather inept way, I tried to give them room to talk; "It seems to me you are doing important work, making a good income. Why would you want to do what I do?"

Then the flood gates would often burst open and I heard such things as,

"You don't know what I have to put up with."
"I don't have the freedom you do."
"It is stifling to build widgets everyday."
"There are things not in textbooks that students ought to know."
"It would be a welcome change to teach students who wanted to listen."
(Little did they know. There are also students who do not want to listen.)

And then almost always, "If you knew what goes on…." This line of conversation would invariably bring up ethical dilemmas faced by good people everyday, that don't get to the media, and about which we don't talk very much. All these conversations struck home and stayed with me as I tried to shape academic programs, as I challenged good faculty to think beyond their discipline as they taught students, and as I taught my own classes. But all the time I kept wondering why men and women continued to pursue careers that made them so unhappy. Just recently, I had a physician tell me, "I want to get out of this *business*, but I don't know what else I would do." What he and many other professionals, including business executives, were saying is something like, "At this stage of my career I can't ask my family to forego the lifestyle they have come to expect." *They felt trapped.*

Gradually, very gradually, it began to sink into my numb skull that many of our company executives, doctors, lawyers, and other professionals were unhappy people who got little satisfaction from their careers. I continue to wonder what this unhappiness has done to our work ethic, productivity, competitiveness, quality of services, and certainly to our moral fiber.

I have also had many conversations with fellow business school deans around the country and learned very early that my experience wasn't unique. One of the most gratifying parts of my job has always been the pleasure I have gotten from business leaders who came to the school to share their experience and knowledge with students and faculty. These highly successful people loved it. As a group, they are giving, caring people. All of my fellow deans have tended to confirm similar contacts with business executives. In retrospect, I think we were also giving them a place to get away, almost as a retreat—to unload.

Do these conversations with business executives and fellow deans constitute a research universe large enough to make generalizations? I believe so, but probably not to the satisfaction of my academic colleagues, since I made no effort to organize a concerted study, develop a system to collect empirical evidence, or to concentrate on it as obsessively as researchers must do. But much has been written in the last 40 to 50 years on the issues revolving around the executive conscience. All these books and articles have also reinforced my evolving sense that we have a serious problem in management both in motivating people to do their best work and in making them aware of what is ethical. My research has been accumulated over 35 years of observation of leadership processes and as a participant in the education of leaders in business.

It would be a mistake to assume that the unspoken ethical issues always emanate from the top. They frequently do, but there is also the problem of middle and lower level managers perpetrating some form of ethical indiscretion, or crime for that matter, and it does not always cause a response from the top, as it should. The result is normalization of poor work habits or, worse, moral sickness. And all too often, the residual effects come home to roost down in the trenches, in lower and middle management offices, where they may go on for years and seldom make the news, even if they are of the moral sickness variety. We see the issues at the top when they make the news, but we never hear about the pain of good people in the middle looking for leadership.

But sometimes the normalization does start at the top, even if for seemingly innocent reasons. A good example of the normalization from the top occurred several years ago in one of our largest manufacturing companies. For several years, the company, an icon in their industry, operated under a policy that told employees to "steal shamelessly." It was intended to urge employees to share ideas and not to be constrained because an idea came from someone else, if it could help the company. As it developed, however, many employees interpreted it literally and stooped to some unethical measures to find out what competitors were doing (industrial espionage). Well, it can happen that one bad apple turns up in the barrel, but it should not have taken years to correct such misguided notions, but it did. It became normalized. This manufacturer was and is a company that prides itself on using professional and ethical management techniques, but even in well-intended good companies, bad habits can and do develop.

After half a century of "professional management," which has been my life's involvement, reality is that by the 1980's most top executives in major corporations had also come up through the ranks of middle managers in large corporations. In other words, senior executives had first learned concepts of professional management in the same morally sterile corporate cultures as their subordinates. They had cut their teeth in the same highly competitive environment of American corporate management. They were products of the "anything goes" systems they now managed. Inbreeding of deep-seated unethical conduct has come full circle. It has become an accepted way of life for too many people who propose to lead us, even in good, highly respected companies.

The Maze of Moral Disinterest

As happened in the large manufacturing company referred to earlier, we have developed a maze of opportunity for unscrupulous and dishonest people who we normally expect to do the right thing as they lead us. Add these to the "usual suspects" who are crooks by nature and we have a maze of leadership failures at all levels and connections in our lives. No, all leaders are not crooks, just a few of them. However, there are all too many who fail to "stand tall," "walk the talk," or simply stand for their convictions. These types of "leaders" stoop to what I call their *passive self-interest,* the tendency to do nothing when something is needed.

Then, there are too many who fail to see the ethical nature of complex decisions about people, prices, sources of supply, and a host of other strategic programs and projects. They become so engrossed in the business decision they lose sight of the "right thing to do." Too many leaders have the competence to lead but the ethics of their decisions gradually get lost over the years through lack of practice.

We can see this throughout society. We can see it in every social and political system we depend upon, i.e. government, business, the professions, education, and even in our personal relationships with one another. We are rapidly losing sight of basic right and wrong, the lack of truth has spawned a disdain for the great institutions of our country, and the moral agent for good conduct (the denominational church) is late entering the fray even in its meager way.

In the pages that follow it is my purpose to describe the maze of moral disinterest. Other books address ethical topics by focusing either on issues of compliance with some recognized rule of conduct or on the individual's personal search for good behavior. Both of these efforts are essential and helpful in understanding right from wrong. In addition, however, our society has progressed to a high level of sophistication and complexity that seems at times to have taken on a life of its own and our many systems of life create breeding grounds for mischief. Understand, however, systems are neither moral nor immoral, but they do provide an enabling environment for the unscrupulous. These systems and those who lead within them are the focus of the pages that follow.

◆   ◆   ◆

There is an old bit of truth about building character that also bears on this normalization process:

What we believe determines what we think.
What we think determines what we do.
What we do determines who people think we are.
And what we do repeatedly determines who we really are.

As a society, too many of us have grown up *repeatedly* ignoring the ethics of what we do and, in the process, we normalized a great moral sickness:

* Too many leaders at all levels of society have *repeatedly* ignored the little moral failures around them while they were pursuing self-interested careers or organizational ends with little concern for the means of achieving them. And it is not always intentional, merely a failure to recall the moral choice at the right time.

* Yes, affluence has been a major motivator leaving moral conduct to the poor people. But affluence is only the tip of the iceberg. It has been more of an effect than a cause. One of Gandhi's *Seven Deadly Sins of Modern man* was, "Wealth without Work." I think his observation gets closer to the roots of the problem. Wealth, personal and corporate, has been the goal, leaving the work ethic to people whose only direction was to get results.

* We have systematically and *repeatedly* removed the moral restraints of the church from leaders in business, government, education, and all of society thus resorting to a consensus morality. If the process of building character does truly start with what one believes, we have not given beliefs enough emphasis. We gradually turned the task over to self-serving people who were only interested in the here and now (their here and now!). Christian values were supposed to stay within the walls of the church building, greatly restricting its ability to shape *beliefs*. If one never shapes *beliefs*, he/she never reaches the starting point for determining *character* and moral decadence becomes normalized.

This is good place to define how I will be using the term "church." One would think it is not necessary but apparently there are many interpretations of religious organizations that hold worship and meditation services and who recognize the one God. Then, of course, there are other religions, such as Judaism and Islam, who use other terms to refer to their forms of worship.

By "church", I mean the worldwide congregation of believers who Jesus foresaw when he said to Peter, "And I tell you that you are Peter, and upon this rock I will build my church,…" RSV, Matthew 16:18. Peter had just acknowledged Jesus to be the Son of God. Protestants, of which I am one, believe Jesus referred to Peter's words of recognition, which is where the church receives its authority and power. Therefore, with due deference to my Catholic, Jewish, and Muslim friends, I will use the word "church" in the manner I know best.

While I applaud all the literature addressing ethical issues of lying, cheating, stealing, abusing, and other shoddy ways of treating people, there are still other factors in normalizing unethical, immoral, and even criminal behavior. I have the strong opinion that, in our systematized life, we have created institutions and operating systems that, when taken all together; become enabling factors, if not causal, for the unscrupulous. I am talking about:

* An economic system that nurtures "buy now/pay later,"

* Misuse of the corporate form of business organization that isolates managers from accountability to owners,

* Education of professional managers focused on meeting profit and career objectives with little attention to moral training,

* Gradual acceptance of little ethical indiscretions that do not interfere with a larger purpose, and

* Waning influence of the religious community, particularly in onfronting the misconduct that ultimately make front-page news.

These *enabling factors* are the concern in the pages that follow, without intending to diminish discussion of individual unethical conduct.

◆   ◆   ◆

Religion has had a profound effect on nations, rulers, and leaders since the beginning of recorded time, either by its positive influence or by its failure to influence profound issues such as slavery and mistreatment of Indians. The search for truth has been a major part of people's life goals since the beginning of recorded time. All faiths have been in this battle to regain the moral sense of our leaders. However, I am a Christian, and I am much more at home focusing my arguments from that perspective. Thus, my intended audience is Christian leaders with no offense intended to people of other faiths. Other moral people from other faiths can make similar arguments from their own teachings. I encourage them to do so.

In the fall of 2003, a report from the National Science Foundation provided data to indicate a slight increase in the religiosity of Americans, if you can use church attendance as a barometer. It also reported that 46% of their respondents said they attended church at least once a week. This was much higher than other surveys and it is higher than European countries where only 4% to 12% said they went to church at least once a week. Even with my usual skepticism about surveys, I am heartened by the report. It tells me that many people are looking to their faith for answers to our many social and political leadership problems. If so, it also tells me now is an opportune time to emphasize the role of the church in promoting Christian values and raising the ethical bar for leaders.

This is the goal in the pages that follow as we examine the societal shifts, the leadership failures, the professional management motivations, and the moral voids that have become an integral part of doing business. What has made us morally sick?

1

NORMAL ISN'T WHAT IT USED TO BE

I'll bet Enron, Arthur Anderson, Global Crossings, Tyco, and WorldCom all have had ethics policies in place for many years, long before the Sarbanes-Oxley Act of 2002. Without ethics policies, businesses have great difficulty avoiding their culpability for the torts, security fraud, and other contract infractions of their employees, especially officers. Further, I'll bet most, if not all, of the indicted and charged executives in these companies considered themselves to be highly ethical people (and probably still do). It is also not unreasonable to assume that most of these corporate leaders were reasonably active members of a church (at least contributors).

While I am surmising, I'll go one more step. I'll bet every one of them knew they were breaking the law. And for each of these rogues who made the news, there are many others who haven't yet made the headlines, but who have been "pushing the ethical envelope" too far, compromising the values usually stated in their own ethics policies. Until the 20th century, we, meaning people in the industrialized, democratized world, have never before made such a distinct delineation between conduct in our professional lives and in our personal lives. We have a new phenomenon in history.

Before I get any farther along this road, let me anticipate one point that someone always makes. I know full well, maybe better than most, that not all leaders are bad apples. The barrel still has many good ones, probably the majority, who do indeed try to travel the high road of leadership. But I think a lot of ethical gray areas have developed in the minds of managers. The difference between right and wrong has become clouded by changes in social expectations and a rampant pursuit of economic gain. It is difficult today for any executive, not just the bad ones, to be sure about their decisions and conduct.

How bad is our conduct? How unethical are executives and employees? Innumerable social commentators have presented data on this point. In Appendix A to this chapter, I refer to a few recent ones, but by no means are they the only studies. Consequently, I am hesitant to say they are representative, but they do suggest some of the issues in using them to draw conclusions. Generally, studies over the last 30 to 40 years indicate a long-term deterioration in our moral behavior with some aberrations in the trend after such tragedies as the 9/11 attacks. No rational person can have observed society for the last fifty years without concluding that morality and ethics have gone to "hell in a hand basket." For several generations, leaders who should be setting high standards have been accepting moral standards for the trailing generations that seem to deteriorate more every year.

UNETHICAL ON PURPOSE OR BY DEFAULT

Actually, the world of business leaders is no different from all other social groups, at least when it comes to bad apples. Crooks are everywhere, along with good people who sometimes do bad things. My intuition, from 50 years of observing leaders and from all the literature on the subject, suggests that one can divide society into three groups;

People who are pathological crooks, know it, and don't care	<1%
People who have lost sight of what is unethical or illegal	30%
Good people who occasionally do dishonest things	69%

The percentages are only there for relative emphasis and are only my assessment as a people-watcher. You can easily challenge their preciseness, but I do indeed believe they approximate the magnitude of the moral and ethical problem today. The group of leaders in the second category is the concern of the chapters that follow.

Since the list adds to 100%, I guess I have accepted the Apostle Paul's charge that "all have sinned and fall short of the glory of God." Nobody is perfect but a few are imperfect by choice while others are imperfect out of ignorance or weakness. The world has always had crooks whose sole motivation has been self-interest served by any means, and we always will have such scoundrels. They are the "1% or less" group.

It is the middle group of 30% who are my concern because they offer the best chance of redirecting the ethical values of the business world. They have the power to reduce the skullduggery in corporate offices and in government. Evil deeds don't necessarily make evil people. In this sense, there is hope that we can encourage those whose evil tendencies come from ignorance of *moral standards*. Note that I say *"moral standards,"* not the law. The distinction here might best be understood after reviewing the discussion in Appendix B about such words as *morals* and *ethics*.

Interestingly, many leaders do understand when they evade the law but they have made a clear separation of their business ethics from the standards of the rest of their lives. "Business is business and religion is religion" is ignorance of moral undergirding, even if Cotton Mather, who said it in the 18th century, was a preacher.

Another obvious point that should be acknowledged is that the 2001 scandals were not new. They were the tip of an iceberg that has been floating under murky water for a long time. You have only to review the history of the robber barons of the late 19th Century, price fixing cases that led to a series of anti-trust legislation in the early 20th Century, accounts of scandals in the administration of almost every president we have had (not just Watergate), and even the sad state of affairs in some of our churches in recent days. All these affairs and an avalanche of illegal deeds by some of our most respected corporations and national leaders have led to a broad range of restraining legislation and new laws. But the beat goes on and is getting louder.

Charles Colson, the White House conspirator in Watergate, who is eminently qualified to comment on executive office hanky-panky, talks about his colleagues in crime as victims of a system of internal intrigue with too much power and too few controls over their activities. At first, we thought he was too kind in his analysis of his role and that of his colleagues. We just wanted to write off the crooks by putting them in jail. Rightly so, but in the intervening years, Colson has made a believer out of many of us. The hallowed halls of government are rife with decadent and criminal malcontents who got that way because they were not prepared for the massive power that came to them. Colson seems to have lifted himself out of the stench of government inner sanctum skullduggery without being overly harsh about his buddies, even Nixon. Yes, we must punish the scoundrels, but we also have to change the system of managing government.

About the 2001 corporate office scandals, he said that new laws passed by Congress after all the scandals would have little effect. Watergate, according to Colson, didn't happen because of the lack of laws. He believed they all knew they were breaking the law, that they viewed themselves as good people, but the law in their minds didn't apply to them. None of their conventional community or church involvements stopped them, nor did the law or company or organizational codes of ethics. Ironically, few of Colson's cronies were the type who would steal from widows. They had simply separated the ethics of the White House from that of the rest of their lives. And the problem, even in the Watergate era, was never limited to government. It also reflected an attitude that ran through many corporate offices, universities, non-profits, and other organizations as well and is still gnawing at our moral fiber even as we start the 21st Century.

SO, WHAT IS THE PROBLEM?

What will slow down unscrupulous leaders' headlong search for greedy, unethical, and often illegal wealth, power, or status? If the law, corporate codes, or social conventions are not effective, some way must be found to change leader's propensity to abort the rules of the game as they participate in our free market economy. I have a sinking feeling that we are not only about to destroy our economy but also the concept of an American civilization by the weight of the greed that has driven it in the last fifty years. We don't yet have to throw out the whole barrel of apples but we do need to do a better job of sorting out the rotten ones. You know, you can make good cider out of rotten apples, but they can also spoil all the other apples in the barrel.

The search for morality has been a purpose as far back as we have records. Even Socrates refused to say he knew a "good life" when he saw it. He could only continue to ask questions that led in the direction of *goodness*. Jesus did not leave a list of conducts He considered to be good. Instead, He gave us guidance and measuring sticks to make our own determination. I'm only saying it will take time to re-kindle our sense of Christian values no matter when we choose to start, so why not now? We have to clean up the minds and souls of all who make up our economic and governance systems, the source of the rottenness. We do need to provide moral leadership and if this doesn't raise a call for a stronger, more aggressive, united church, I have completely misread the New Testament.

During the 1980's and 1990's more and more stories began to reach the media about unethical and illegal conduct within corporate walls. That much was not a new phenomenon but the crescendo became deafening as we entered the 21st Century. The major violations made the news but they didn't begin to touch the embedded systemic misconduct that never surfaced. Why? I guess little indiscretions just weren't big enough for Peter Jennings, Tom Brokaw, Dan Rather, or Judy Woodruff. Actually, there was more to it. The media wants to report law-breakers, not sinners. They know what we want to hear. OK, let's turn it around. We ought to know what turns the media on. We have no reason to expect three minutes on the evening news to be used to report unethical behavior in middle management. Newspapers are not going to put such stories on the front page either.

But I think there is still more to it. We can also sense that little indiscretions were not worthy of much attention inside big businesses themselves. No one is calling on business executives to put down sin, only unethical and criminal acts. They certainly aren't going to put much energy into "sin control," compared with the larger goals of the business plan. Many people would say it was the larger profit motive that caused so many companies to normalize routine mischief. True, but this far too simplistic. It has more to do with job security, management by objective, the career ladder, a highly competitive internal technostructure, and the challenge of the family's "good life," none of which creates much concern about rightness and wrongness. And, yes, the "bottom line" is an imperative for managers who have been assigned growth, return on investment, and profit targets.

But let's be fair. It's also about who will be the judge of right and wrong. Leadership in all facets of life is under suspicion today. The distinction has come down to consensus of some subset of society. Deviations from God's will don't get much hearing in corporate America and, let's face it, there are wide ranging views today on what is God's will. Frankly, I think it is more about mere humans trying to make what we want to do fit into God's will. It won't work.

Wait! There is still more. We call ourselves a Christian nation with deep roots in the church. If so, why don't Biblical teachings provide some moral direction to tough individualistic corporate executives who struggle to know the "right thing" to do? They do, but we have to understand Biblical teachings and interpolate them to the office. This means executives, like all of us, must study them. Demands of the organization and its systems absorb our thinking and cloud our understanding of right and wrong. There was a time when the church-going community tended to "keep an eye" on business transactions as it did all other aspects of life. Really, they did! Business dealings, even as late as the 1930's, were a barometer of an entrepreneur's moral life. Can you believe this? But businesses got much bigger, with widely dispersed places of business and more complex organizations and operating procedures while church influence gradually waned. The reasons we attribute to this process depend upon one's attitude about religion and its relevance to the workaday world. I certainly don't want to revert to the church-dominated tyranny of the Holy Roman Empire or the Inquisition systems of the Middle Ages, but I do think we have gone too far in the other direction of a passive milk-toast church out on the fringes of society. There is still a place, a need, for an influential church *that speaks with one voice;* a strong moral voice in the land. While we are dreaming, we might as well dream big.

Historically, business leaders, especially successful ones, have been "individualistic," meaning they don't necessarily follow conventional wisdom. Their drive for success is a genuine American trait that executives around the world have attempted to imitate. It is directly from our past, and we should continue to work hard to develop more individuality today. With adequate restraints, it's a good thing. But, part of my concern is that maybe we aren't as individualistic as we present ourselves, or as we once were. John Kenneth Galbraith, in his 1960's book, *The New Industrial State,* talked about a technostructure in industry. He was talking about our large businesses which were really run by a mass of middle managers whose sole ambition was to please their bosses. His main point was about declining efficiency of decision making, but he was also making another point, that the systems of industry were leading the decision making process rather than leaders. This has much to do with the decline in moral leadership. Unethical conduct, as well as inefficiency, can get buried in the maze of corporate systems.

It is also true in smaller companies that individuality of the entrepreneur isn't what we think. I have listened to many small business owners decry government control while they enjoyed SBA or FMHA loans, payroll subsidies for minority or handicapped workers, federal contracts set aside for small businesses, etc. It seems like many of them want free enterprise for their competitors and socialism for themselves.

However, Galbraith made a valid observation that the new technocrats in large corporations were judged by their bosses almost completely upon their contribution to their component of the business plan. *How* middle managers met the objectives was not of primary importance in too many companies. He wasn't addressing the moral decay in the country so much as our declining corporate productivity and creativity of the 60's. But I think the motivations that weighed down the ability of companies to compete also contributed heavily to the moral indifference of the last half century. Let's be clear. These "boss satisfying" tactics in business are also evident in other forms of endeavor, even in government. Incidentally, think about the fact that in affairs of government ultimately we, the people, become the boss. Have we given proper instruction to our hired help?

When I make such sweeping statements, I feel compelled to say again that I know there are many companies who try to operate ethically, even by Christian standards. In some companies, however, managers with whom I have talked often refer to times when they or their colleagues simply failed to recognize unethical, even illegal, issues faced by lower level managers because of company well-intended plans or policies. The extremely important point, worth repeating, is that unethical or illegal acts in large organizations are not necessarily the work of bad apples. More often than not, they result from inaction at times when moral beliefs were being challenged; doing nothing when something was needed. It is what I call the *passive self-interest* by leaders who put moral considerations on the shelf, at least until Sunday morning. It may be that careers are at stake, that moral understanding is lacking, or sometimes inaction is the better part of valor when dishonesty is in fact intended.

NORMAL IS JUST A HABIT

Then, one day in on the early 1980's, I heard a fellow academician make an observation that rang the bell and gave me a starting place to answer my question about why we have seen a steady erosion of morality in our businesses, and in the whole country. He said, "*Every society normalizes its own sickness.*"

I first heard it from Frederick Herzberg, who at that time was a professor at the University of Utah, psychologist, management writer, and consultant. I don't know if it was original with him but it seemed to provide a nucleus of truth to bring together a number of nagging concerns that had haunted me for years. It launched me on a search for its meaning because I thought it might have something to do with why so many business leaders felt so little concern for little moral mischief, even though we and they know it is habit forming. We know that the crooks who make the news have not committed a crime or moral indiscretion for the first time in their lives. It just doesn't happen that way. Dr. Herzberg's idea led me to a logical adaptation to the moral issue in our country:

Every society normalizes its own (moral) sickness.

Gradually it occurred to me that more time needs to be spent trying to prevent the misbehavior that is less than life-threatening but more infectious. We have lots of people writing volumes on oil spills by drunken tanker captains in Alaska, Arab-Israeli confrontation, and, in the United States, campaign financing, abortion, sexual exploitation, and the morality of war; and each topic deserves all the attention it gets. No question about it!

As crucial as these great issues were and still are, however, I have convinced myself, if no one else, that our best way of addressing immoral leadership which contributes heavily to these great issues is through *early intervention*. This latter phrase is a euphemism for let's nip the buds of misbehavior at home, in schools, and in churches before the habit of misbehavior becomes engrained. Each of these associations is a society in itself, but a society will also include the highly sophisticated systems of corporate America, government, and any other large organization.

We're talking about education, but not just education for the purpose of socialization or competence. It speaks loudly for moral education based upon Christian principles. If this sounds familiar and naïve to you, consider the possibility that you may have become acclimated, like all of us, to the corporate way of life that brought us to this affluent point in our lives. It happened to me and I was never employed by a large corporation. I only taught it, encouraged it, and consulted with managers who were part of large corporations, but I was not alone. In other words, *you, too, may have become a complete organization person.*

Over my lifetime, I have watched the weakening of our feeble grip on morality, ethical conduct, and character. But even the weak grip seems to have given way in recent times and I have the strong feeling that it is because our feeble effort to develop character and promote ethical conduct are without reference to any form of higher power. In fact, the law or political correctness in the United States at this point stifles efforts to use any form of higher power to establish right and wrong for any purpose outside the church or home and neither of these time-honored institutions is a pillar of moral strength today, leaving us only with *consensus ethics*. By consensus ethics, I mean right or wrong determined by society itself, by legislative action, by codes established by group participation or based upon what others do, and by law based upon precedence or on liberal interpretations of the Constitution. The farther we have allowed law, social customs, ordinances, and codes of conduct to stray from the ultimate source of moral authority, God, the faster our standards of conduct have deteriorated. This was Socrates problem 2500 years ago. He kept questioning what a moral life looked like and gradually came to the conclusion that there was need to identify and accept a higher power in one's search for righteousness.

So, *consensus* tools have not deterred the rising incidents of misbehavior because there is no *universally accepted* source of authority. Supreme Court decisions have the force of the federal government but there are still numerous examples of people who do not accept them or who spend their time looking for loopholes. And worse yet, court decisions are now based upon their interpretation of consensus attitudes in our country. What is moral is not determined in courts, Congress, or by the President's executive orders (Democrat or Republican), and was not intended to be. It isn't supposed to be! Every person's life is fulfilled from their obligation to search for their own morality, but not without moral training. It's about education, folks.

Is it right to send women into situations that are potentially unsafe or which lead to promiscuous conduct? Who says promiscuity is immoral to begin with? What's so bad about divorce and abortion? Why is it wrong to pay 21 year olds millions of dollars to play basketball, football, soccer, or baseball? Why is bribery so terrible? Is it wrong to put out advertising material that, while it may not be a lie, leads to incorrect decisions by consumers? And then, what's so bad about stock options for executives only? If these socially visible matters are complex, what about the corporate strategy of downsizing or closing a division simply because its annual profit is not growing? You get the picture.

I have been a critic of certain denominations of the church (including my own) for a long time because of their relative ineffectiveness in addressing everyday ways of unethical and often illegal conduct. Putting it as diplomatically as I can, it seems to me that the church has been something less than a force in subduing unethical conduct, to say nothing of the burgeoning crime rate. But I am probably too harsh when I expect ministers to know in detail what enters into the daily decision-making processes of large corporations. Why should they know when leaders within business seem incapable of tracking their own decadence (or at least unwilling to try)? And let's not forget that while ministers may be leaders, they can only lead when we parishioners will follow. Churches are still organizations of volunteers. Remember?

NORMAL, ELUSIVE WITH DIFFERENT STROKES FOR DIFFERENT FOLKS

Recently my eye doctor told me my vision was normal. He was kind enough not to add, "for someone your age." I have had cataracts removed from both eyes. My un-blurred vision lasts about 20 minutes when I'm reading and I can't follow my golf ball further than 150 yards. All this is apparently normal for senior citizens. I have this theory that, short of a fatal accident, we leave this world one body part at a time. This, too, seems to be normal. My vision would surely not be normal for a 25 year old.

All of this is to say, normal is relative. Spending money in government faster than we receive tax revenues is normal today. This has made it normal for elected officials to offer their constituents an ever-increasing share of the government pie. None of this was normal until the mid-thirties. It is normal for affluent people to take trips in airplanes, even in times of recession, but it is not normal at anytime for those who live in poverty. But these lifestyle activities are obvious. We should also be concerned about the long list of normal immoral lifestyle activities today that have become rampant in the last half century.

Earlier I said one aspect of my job as dean in several university business schools during much of the last half of the 20th century turned out to be listening to hundreds of business managers and some political leaders, people who wanted to express some of their inner concerns about their work and responsibilities. This activity wasn't on my job description, but it led to some of the most interesting learning experiences of my career. I was especially affected by so many whose concerns were about the moral failures they saw in their companies and by those who acknowledged that their lucrative careers had not been as satisfying as they had hoped. It gradually dawned on me that big business had created a culture in which too many participants questioned the ethics of their company or fellow executives and sometimes worried about the legality of what they were doing themselves. Yet, they felt trapped by lifestyles, family interests, financial strangulation, and ego.

What am I saying? The mischief we eventually heard about through the media which has infected business has:

- *Infected all of our great institutions: business, government, education, the professions, even the churches,*

- *Has been growing, seething unobtrusively in all these institutions as today's leaders paid their dues in the trenches over the last 50 years (at least) on their way to the executive office.*

But not enough was done about it early in this tragic development. *We have normalized leadership mischief!* Too many of us have gone about our self-focused sense of the "here and now" with little regard for a God-focused moral high ground. I don't agree with everything Charlton Heston says but I do understand what he meant when he spoke to the Harvard Law School in 1999. "Disobedience is in our DNA. We feel innate kinship with the disobedient spirit of those who tossed tea into Boston Harbor, who sent Thoreau to jail, who refused to sit in the back of the bus, and who protested a war in Vietnam." Are we losing our sense of individual dissent?

We should have felt moral indignation long ago about the little things leaders did (or failed to do) that kept driving us down the road to the moral decadence in today's society. We should have resisted more strongly the tendency to become *normal.*

Not being a sociologist, philosopher, or anthropologist, I simply want to share some thoughts as a Christian observer of the business world's leaders from my desk in the dean's office. I am focusing on business leaders at this point, but not exclusively, because it's a field I know a little about and also because their failures are also found throughout all of our institutions. No discerning person thinks the ethical dilemma we face today can be laid solely on the desk of business executives. I think we have normalized some lousy moral leadership throughout society in the last half century. By the way, if you want to remind me that "people who live in glass houses shouldn't throw stones" you have more cause than you know. My own self-satisfied career during the last half of the 20th century kept me from writing this book long ago. I am a product of a morally complacent half century. But then who is going to write it? Jesus still isn't writing for publication.

When our forefathers signed the Declaration of Independence, it was not normal. When Washington's soldiers chose to stay the winter at Valley Forge, it was not normal. When settlers left home to go west, it was not normal. The Civil War was not normal; the Brown vs. the Topeka Board of Education decision was not normal. Pearl Harbor was not normal, nor was the massive response to it during WWII. The attacks on 9/11/01 were the first on the continental US since 1865, and clearly they were not normal. And the response of millions of people who wanted to help was not normal.

The economic growth of our country has been achieved by people accepting abnormal risks (yes, and sometimes they used unethical and illegal methods). The greatness of America has always been stimulated by normal people achieving unusual success from abnormal efforts. In earlier days, we called it "rugged individualism" and, with all its warts and sores, it was this unique American quality that enabled us to grow into the world superpower. Today, we call this character trait one of the qualities of the American civilization. Calling the nation to *normal* conduct won't keep us on top, it won't prepare us for the fight with terrorism, and it certainly won't restore our moral fiber.

To do the things we normally do sounds so comfortable—so *normal.* To go through our normal routine each day gives us a sense that we are well anchored. President Bush knew this because shortly after the terrorist attacks on 9/11/01 he made a big point about not allowing our *normal* lives to be disrupted. After the attacks and the anthrax scares Americans were urged to keep on with activities that would continue to fuel a red hot economy. We were asked to take a trip (on an airplane!), go to the beach, spend money, and do all the things Americans always do. Maybe it was a bit "tongue in cheek" but it's clear that if we had drawn back in our spending habits, our economy might have dropped off the charts. Nevertheless, I'm still not sure about this business of normalizing America.

History is full of examples of great empires and people whose downfall resulted directly from normalizing decadent immoral qualities. Rome rose to power through great military strength and expertise in government, but fell as its pursuit of a decadent lifestyle eroded its greatness. Greece, noted for its intellectual leadership, faded because wealthy leaders resorted to slave labor to do menial work while they sat around listening to great orators and discussing philosophy and poetry. Great Britain's history in India was riddled with episodes of immoral treatment of the Indian people. The United States is trying hard now to remove the blot of slavery as well as the mistreatment of Indians. Our success in doing so may well determine whether or not we continue as the great world power. More about this later.

APPENDIX A

Universities, at least the good ones, require faculty to be involved in some form of research to expand the body of knowledge in their disciplines. In business schools and all the social sciences, this research creates an enormous demand for information that is almost always collected by empirical studies, i.e. surveys. Guess who bears the brunt of the business questionnaires? Business executives. I often felt it was like unleashing the hounds on the poor fox.

Nevertheless, results of these surveys end up being published somewhere. Since the 1970's, the number one topic of business empirical research has been business ethics. In addition, there have been innumerable research organizations spawned that also undertake studies, offer workshops and courses, and generally inform us about their findings. All these researchers have created an enormous body of knowledge from their work on business ethics.

In general, I accept the totality of the research since the magnitude of the ethical problems in business and government reported is not substantially different. Even so, several typical studies and their findings can illustrate the nature of their emphasis on consensus ethics.

One such survey was the periodic study of 1,500 major companies by the Ethics Resource Center, *2003 National Business Ethics Survey*. The last study was in 2000. In comparing results, several generalizations were offered.

—Respondents in the 2003 study were much more sensitive to ethical conduct resulting from such national trauma as the 9/11 terrorist attacks, the anthrax scares, the dot com crash, the scandals uncovered in corporate offices, the enactment of the Sarbanes-Oxley Act of 2002, etc.

—Respondent's reports of observed misconduct dropped from 31% in 2000 to 22% in 2003.

—However, one-third of the respondents said their co-workers condone misconduct by showing respect for offenders who achieve success.

—Managers under age 30 are twice as likely to feel pressure and succumb to unethical behavior as older managers. In addition, only 43% of younger managers are likely to report observed misconduct compared to 69% of all other employees.

Another study of 2,795 employees in a wide range of industries was the *2001 National Employee Benchmark Study,* by WalkerInformation. Some of their findings include;

—54% of respondents reported observations of ethical violations in the past 2 years. Some of the infractions reported were;

Lying to supervisors	26%
Lying on reports/falsifying records	18%
Unfair treatment of employees	26%
Improper use of company assets	21%
Conflict of interest	20%
Stealing	19%
Sexual harassment	15%

—Incidents of ethical violations varied widely among industries with retail businesses reporting the highest percentages. Financial, Technology, and Insurance companies showed the lowest percentages.

The Business Research Laboratory conducted a third on-line study in May, 2003. While they do not provide detail about the size of their sample or the types of questions, they do summarize these interesting conclusions about how employees rated their employers:

Extremely Unethical	5.13%
Very Unethical	10.77%
Somewhat unethical	15.90%
Somewhat ethical	21.54%
Very ethical	30.77%
Extremely ethical	15.90%

Several generalizations jump out at you from these studies. First, the sensitivity to unethical and illegal conduct was much higher immediately after the trauma of 2001 and 2002. All of a sudden, it was patriotic to be good. This is usually the case. The Great Depression brought on deeper interest in religion. So did the Pearl Harbor attack and the threat of nuclear war over Cuba in 1962. But as we regained our sense of well-being, we become less concerned with ethics and morality.

A second generalization comes from the finding that younger managers are more susceptible to pressure to do mischief than older executives. I believe this strongly and will reinforce this observation more forcefully in later chapters. At this juncture, it speaks to the point I want to make that early intervention offers our best hope for reducing the motivation to mischief. But even these findings are not enough. Consider the innumerable studies on campuses that have told us that as many as 75% of all students cheat on examinations, plagiarize papers, and, in other ways, subvert the systems intended to give them a quality education.

Third, the studies give us different percentages about workers' observations of misconduct from 22% to 54%. In other studies, it is often even higher. But in some studies, the question is also asked if the respondent has committed unethical acts. Invariably the percentage is much lower. What else should we expect? It does, however, caution us against relying too heavily on the absolute numbers in any one study. Don't let empirical studies, even by competent researchers, displace common sense that comes from observing the world around you.

Finally, people respond to questionnaires about ethical conduct based upon their own understanding of good conduct. Occasionally, the researcher may define what is meant by unethical conduct but most often it is left to the respondent's interpretation. If our world is gradually drifting toward a consensus ethic condoning right/wrong by popular demand, we can justly question what the surveys are telling us. They certainly do not compare everyday conduct with Biblical teachings, Judaic Law, or the Koran.

APPENDIX B

There are some words and phrases that are important in the pages that follow, philosophical though they may be. Allow me to take a short excursion into the world of philosophers and try to explain how these words will be used throughout this book. Remember, I am neither a philosopher nor a theologian.

MORALITY

For Socrates, *morality* was a life-long and life-ending search. He wanted to know what makes one's life worthwhile. What was a good life? He kept asking his questions until Athenian officials had enough. They thought he was putting them down. They grew tired of his questions and finally told him to shut up and drink his hemlock. Actually, he chose his own method of demise but the alternatives were much worse.

But Socrates' wisdom has outlived him all these centuries. He thought there should be a balance between concern for self and concern for others. It does have a familiar ring to Bible readers. It sounds strangely like, "Do unto others what you would have them do unto you." He was a promoter of character, as are ethicists today. He came to believe good character and morality were determined by the constant search for balance between selfishness and selflessness. Umm? Don't let this idea go by without noting that it not only encourages a life that does no harm or an absence of bad conduct. It also calls us to take positive steps to do good for others.

Socrates also believed everyone possessed a soul, and he believed in the importance of knowledge and true wisdom as essential to the properly tended soul. He also acknowledged the need for a higher power in order for men to draw on in their search, but, alas, Greek society did not have one higher power. They worshipped many gods which left a void that Socrates was unable to fill.

Starting with Socrates' concept of *morality,* other philosophers have continued to massage his questions. Even today, morality seems to come from all those endeavors that make life worthwhile and, believe me, it is a constant search. This latter point is something I do know about. To Socrates, even drinking hemlock was worthwhile and moral, because it enabled him to stand up for his beliefs. It made his life worthwhile. It put *self* in the right perspective, for him.

ETHICS

The trouble with Socrates was that he taught using the Socratic Method. He kept asking questions and leaving students (or anyone who would listen) to answer them. This is a form of inductive learning—starting with what is known and moving to logical conclusions about the previously unknown. It's now a time-honored teaching method and my preferred method of teaching. Once I was upbraided by a student when I returned his question with a question (like Socrates!). He was upset because I expected him to think. Looking back at his academic background, perhaps I should have apologized. He had never encountered the Socratic method of filling the void in his brain. He wasn't accustomed to thinking.

A couple of Socrates' followers, Plato and Aristotle, did try to answer his many questions by pressing for a means of determining *what made up a good life*. How do you know it when you see it? Ah, there's the rub in our consensus-driven society. What endeavors could one undertake to create a worthwhile, moral, good life? His two students continued Socrates' search for a universal set of standards which could be used to measure the morality of a life. They did, indeed, contribute to our understanding of what is a good life, but neither they nor anyone else has determined a universal set of standards for all mankind. The search for standards is generally called *ethics*; the study of, or the search for, those standards with which to measure a moral life.

NORMATIVE ETHICS

The quest for standards has continued all these years and has evolved into *normative ethics,* which may be stated simply as a set of standards for a moral life, but usually with reference to a particular aspect of life. Today, it has branched into standards of conduct adopted by diverse groups of people with special interests in its application to their fields of work: businesses, government, schools and universities, the professions, and all types of organizations wanting to establish minimum standards of conduct for employees, students and faculty, citizens, professionals, and everybody under their influence.

Plato and Aristotle seemed to believe that their philosophy of ethics was to be for a Greek society which accepted many gods, as did Socrates, their teacher. One of the questions for western civilization has been whether Greek concepts of morality and normative ethics could be transferred to all societies. It could not, even though we have learned much about a moral life from the early Greek philosophers. No set of standards, laws, codes, or even social conventions can be imposed upon people who think differently, then or today. The absence of authority to impose standards made the good work of Socrates, Plato, Aristotle, and other secular philosophers incapable of universal acceptance even by good-minded people. And this has been true even though the standards among the world's people who seemingly think differently are not all together different. The three Greek philosophers, along with many others, contributed greatly to our concepts of morality and ethics by their searches for a worthwhile life, but they could not generalize their ideas for the whole world.

CHRISTIAN ETHICS

The great attraction of Christianity comes from the recognition of one God as our higher power and from the freedom of every Christian to individually search for what is good, *once they accept the example and teaching of Christ for guidance.*

This leads into an important concept, which is one of the concerns of this book;-*Christian ethics.* What is different about *Christian ethics?*

First, it is what *Christians* believe, not Muslims, Jews, early Greeks, or people of other faiths, although there is much commonality.

Second, it doesn't rest upon any documented set of laws, codes, or conventions although it acknowledges the need for good laws.

Third, it results from an individual, personal love for one's fellow man along with a constant search for Christ's idea of a worthwhile life.

Finally, it is based upon a revealed model for a good life *exemplified and taught* by Jesus Christ, not an imposed way of life.

What Socrates believed about the soul was confirmed by Christ and proven by His resurrection, which was His way of demonstrating to us the ultimate meaning of a good life. Socrates drank hemlock and died because it made his life worthwhile. Jesus was crucified, but rose from the dead, which emphasized his truth as the universal means for all of us to experience a worthwhile life. But Jesus went on to say that we can't earn eternity with God by living worthwhile lives. God can give it to us, but we can't earn it. If so, then what is the value of the standards of Plato, Aristotle, or even Christ in our search for morality? What is *ethical?* What's the point of it all?

When God came and walked among us, he gave us a *model,* not a standard or a set of laws, and, along with the model, he gave us individual *choice* and challenged us to surpass minimum standards of behavior of the law. While we are not challenged by laws, civility and order demand that we have laws, codes, and conventions, and obey them. Christians choose to obey the good laws and work within the law to change the bad ones. Neither are we forced to follow Christ's example, to be moral. Again, we are free to choose to do so or not. The interaction of laws, including moral law and natural law, with our freedom to choose, demands that Christians have the *moral wisdom* to manage the daily struggle. Through the constant development of our *moral wisdom,* we learn to do good for people simply because we love them, not out of any sense of obligation.

Moving from this understanding of our life's struggle on earth, we begin to see or sense that *moral wisdom* is not something we learn from social expedience or necessity or even from good laws, codes, and conventions. We discern *moral wisdom* by constantly asking, "What would Jesus do?" I was deeply affected by the book, *Payne Stewart,* written by his wife, Tracey Stewart, shortly after his death, about his life and his relentless struggle in his later years with the search for *moral wisdom.* I was so affected because I enjoy golf, probably too much. I was particularly impressed with the episode in the book when Payne agreed to wear the bracelet from his son, Aaron, which said, "WWJD." It stood for, "What Would Jesus Do?"

It was an outgrowth of Charles Sheldon's book, *In His Steps,* which had affected so many people. Payne was willing to say to the world that he was on a mission to live the *Christian ethic.* If for no other reason, he wanted to show his son that he believed it to be important. However, because of Payne's witness, many other professional golfers began wearing the bracelet and, from their willingness to do it, the impact of the bracelet grew to other professional athletes and to many other people. This is what I mean when I say we must discern Christian ethics *by seeing it in action in other people.* Why did we have Payne Stewart with us? To play golf? No, I don't think so. To model, as best he could, what Jesus would do.

Christian ethics are different because they are *revealed* in each of us, by each of us, to each of us as *moral wisdom,* rather than being imposed by law, even if that law is *moral law* from God. "God who walked among us" provided the model, the basis, for our life-long moral search—our authority.

Thus, Christian ethics can be said to be the pursuit of a worthwhile life which is a life-long struggle to be like Jesus. It is not necessarily a life like Jesus'; at least it has not been yet. It is the growing realization that a good life is as Socrates said, the life that has a good balance between concern for self and concern for others, but now with an exemplary life of one who achieved it—Jesus Christ. I've not always understood this. It is still a search just as someone once said, "Whoever searches for God has already found him."

Some years ago, I was conducting a leadership ethics workshop for ministers to help them understand the work-a-day life of the business executive. During a discussion of several case studies, one young minister became frustrated with our discussion and blurted out, "I believe in Jesus Christ, crucified and resurrected. That's all I need."

At that moment, he seemed to be off on a tangent so I worked to get discussion "back on the track" of ethical policies in business. Even though I had been pointing out the dangers of consensus ethics, I had not thought far enough ahead to offer a better alternative. The young minister was doing that in his way. He wasn't as naïve as some people, including me, thought. We do need to understand Christian ethics and that they are what was exemplified and taught by Jesus Christ. Believing the great sacrifice of Jesus makes the understanding of Christian ethics much easier.

It sounds as if I am offering Christianity as the panacea for all the world's ills. To a degree, I am. So why hasn't Christianity fulfilled its mission? Perhaps history hasn't completely played out on this matter. But even so, why don't all Christians understand their responsibility to others? Why don't we accept the good life as Christ's followers? Why are we going backwards in our faith journey and in our commitment to Christ's example and teachings? Tough questions! They have much to do with the decaying state of morality in our world today. These are some of the ideas that are to be developed as you read through the pages that follow.

It's a lonely search if you look only to colleagues, fellow workers, friends, or even family for the answers. Walk with God, too, as you walk through the pages that follow.

2

EVERY PERSON A NEIGHBOR

While the background of the normalizing process for moral sicknesses is important, and we will look at some of the background issues, it is also important that we recognize symptoms that infect our personal daily lives. "Every society" can mean a school, our workplace, our neighborhood, a city, state, or country. It can be our circle of friends or our families. For wrongdoing to become normal, someone in a leadership position must choose to do nothing when some action or response is needed. In some way, the leaders rationalize that no action is called for. Even in the allegorical story of creation, we read of the serpent rationalizing God's commandment to Eve.

> But the serpent said to the woman, you will not die (if you eat of the tree of knowledge). For God knows that when you eat of it your eyes will be opened and you will be like God knowing good and evil. So when the woman saw that the tree was good for food, and that it was a delight to the eyes, and that the tree was to be desired to make one wise, she took of its fruit and ate, and also gave some to her husband. (Gen. 3: 5-6, RSV)

It's a story from a writer trying to explain why people want to determine good and evil without God, to illustrate how sin begins, why we are so anxious to be like other people, or why we think no harm will come if we ignore the right thing to do. Note how the story progresses to a position in which Adam and Eve defy their Creator in order to experience pleasure. It's a story about beginnings that has been acted out in the Biblical revelation and in all of life ever since. The writer of Genesis knew well how we could normalize a moral sickness: simply by allowing ourselves to believe that *everybody does it or that God is wrong (or not looking)*.

Our desire to be liked, to be accepted, to be relieved of stress, to have a good life, or just to be happy can be used by unscrupulous people to lead us down the path to normalizing our own personal sicknesses. Once criminals, hucksters, media programmers, sports publicists, self-centered bosses, politicians, and dozens of conniving crooks and con artists know what drives us, they've got us. They know how to use that knowledge to get at us, to separate us from our wealth, to cause us stress, to use us for their own purposes, and, what is most serious, to challenge our moral underpinnings. Hugh Hefner used men's sexual desires to rationalize his brand of self-fulfillment and make it a moral right. He, as much as anyone, made the sexual revolution the norm for the last two generations. To avoid pain or to experience pleasure, too many of us allow ourselves to be led down paths toward normalcy. Conform! Do what everybody else does! It's a serious problem in corporate offices (and everywhere else).

But there is another aspect of this normalization process which is even more insidious and which is usually the starting point for people who find themselves the perpetrators of much greater moral failures. What we do when alone is a good measure of one's character. You've heard this before, but it's true. If we bend when no one is looking, it creates a mindset for doing mischief anytime it is in our self-interest and that makes us susceptible to others with mischief on their minds. The person who first takes a few paper clips, who takes long lunch hours, who talks badly about others, who goes with the crowd, or who does a thousand little mischievous things never would believe they could be led to commit major crimes, but some are. The process of doing the little misdeeds grows with each new one until it is too late and the road back to a moral life is too long.

Invariably, if we could look back over the life of each wrongdoer, we would find a point along the road when someone might have prevented it. Someone who at the right moment could have exercised a little leadership and kept a family member, a friend, an employee, or just a passerby from committing an unethical, maybe even an illegal, deed.

Put the progression in evil tendencies in the context of leaders' *passive self-interest,* a motivation to do nothing when something is needed, and you have a ripe environment for deviant ethical behavior. *Every society normalizes its own sicknesses* because some who purport to be leaders take the *passive self-interest* approach of doing nothing when positive intervention is needed. Too many people who lead tend to restrict their leadership to a narrow field of conduct spelled out in a job description. Good leaders are extremely objective oriented. This is what makes them what they are. Business leaders concentrate on carrying out the business plan, politicians are much too concerned about votes (but they have to be), teachers focus on their subject matter or the process of teaching, parents are often swept up by family financial issues to the exclusion of children's moral growth, even good ministers see their duty as offering good sermons, ministering to needs, and teaching Bible study programs to satisfy a "normalized" congregation. They are all doing their jobs and each has important worthy purposes.

But leaders always have another purpose: *to provide moral leadership.* Too many leaders fail to recognize their position of respect. They don't always see that what they do or allow outside their job description is also indicative to followers of what they will do within their job description. When small infractions do occur, too many leaders look the other way using the guise of focusing on the greater good of their organizations.

This characterization can be carried too far and become a bit unfair, but it is just too easy to fall prey to the normalization of unethical conduct. No, it is not unfair to expect leaders to focus on those things that contribute to a moral workplace, not merely short-term annual performance reviews. Short-term measurements of results *alone* tend to reduce concerns about little ethical infractions especially by leaders whose *passive self-interests* are always near the surface. If it ain't broke, don't fix it.

Too few of us worry about moral training of those we lead until some traumatic crime or ethical infraction occurs. Do you recall President Clinton agreeing to submit to counseling by the two ministers? It was a little late, don't you think? Where was his moral training when he was driving around Arkansas in a carpet bed pick-up? It was certainly too late when he used the oval office for his mischief.

Cain's great question was for all moral people, "Am I my brother's keeper?" Those whose faith gives them the foundation for a moral life know that the resounding answer to Cain is, "yes." No effective leader can believe otherwise, and we are all leaders at some point. Among all else this may mean, it certainly means we are to keep our brothers and sisters from harming themselves. If one believes that religion is irrelevant to the conduct of our lives, then we can ignore Cain's question and continue our self-centered approach to life without concern for the moral condition of those we lead. But if one professes to be a Christian, a follower of Christ, your leadership is also part of your commitment to your faith.

Let me reinforce the earlier point that leaders are not necessarily those at the top of the organization chart. They are where you find them in all kinds of involvements that require them to help someone else. Let me illustrate with a few examples "outside the box."

OUR MORAL SENSE, A WORK IN PROGRESS

My wife and I have two grandsons whom we like to visit at every opportunity. On one such visit when Bailey was 4 and Will was 6, I was left with them while everyone else was out of the house. I was watching a Braves game on TV (and dozing) while the two boys played peacefully (trust me!) with their toys on opposite sides of the family room. After an hour or so, Will got up quietly, went to Bailey's pile of toys, and took one over to his side of the room.

Well, every parent will anticipate the mayhem that followed. "It's mine. I want it," yelled Bailey. Will came back, "You've had it all day. I want it now." Now that was a terrible dilemma for someone who planned to write a book about ethical leadership. What was I to do? I'm only the grandparent.

Each of the boys was exercising his untrained *moral sense*. Bailey believed that because the toy was his, he had property rights and no one else had a right to take it. Will believed that just because he wanted it he should be able to take it. It was an age-old struggle between the "haves" and the "have nots." Besides, Will was bigger (which brought to mind the "survival of the fittest" mentality of the Stone Age). I was taken by surprise so I did what teachers do. I stalled to get more time. Finally, it hit me that I was witness to a clash of two undeveloped moral senses. I wish I had thought of this when I was a parent.

I asked the obvious conciliatory questions. To Will: "Would you want someone to come and take your toys?" "No, but I want to play with it for a little while." Ah ha! There was a meeting ground, "a little while."

I asked Bailey, who has always been the gentle-hearted one, "Aren't you playing with another toy? Can you let your brother borrow one for *a little while*?"

"Well, yes but I want it back."

So we agreed on a half-hour as reasonable time for the toy to be in Will's pile.

War had been averted, they had found a way to share, and I got back to the Braves game. Not quite! About every two minutes, Bailey came to me and whispered, "Is it a half hour yet?" My grandfatherly patience was being sorely tested. There is a limit to this ethics stuff, especially when the Braves are on the tube. It would have been a good time to exercise my *passive self-interest*. No, there are times when we can and should help people avoid ethical dilemmas without expecting perfection.

◆   ◆   ◆

A few years ago, I walked into the typically drab lobby of a manufacturing plant to meet with a friend who was plant manager. There were no pictures on the walls, but there were information and direction signs everywhere—too many, I think, to achieve the hoped for effect. One sign right over the receptionist's desk read "NO SMOKING" in big red letters. It was a simple and familiar message we all see regularly.

I wouldn't have given it a second thought if the receptionist and a man I knew to be the plant superintendent had not been enjoying their conversation, which didn't seem to be about business, and both were smoking. Their lack of concern for the sign wouldn't have bothered me except the plant manager had invited me to come and chat with him about some ideas on leadership ethics. Now I was confronted with an ethical issue in his plant even before I got to his office. I have sorted through a lot of human conduct over the years to enable me to recognize misbehavior when I see it (even my own). The two employees were ignoring the rules, but what about my own responsibility? Could I "look the other way" knowing that *everybody does it?*

What I did was to announce myself as a visitor to see their boss, then look up slowly at the "No Smoking" sign, and return my eyes to the receptionist and then to the superintendent. The result was the quick disappearance of the superintendent and the receptionist mashing her cigarette into the ash tray. Mission accomplished! Well, not quite.

You see, I had used the old adage, "Every society normalizes its own moral sickness," in a discussion group that included the plant manager. He was proud of his company's ethics emphasis and thought he could see opportunities to apply the concept. He wanted to talk about it. Now there I was, about to discuss this little bit of philosophy with a man who believed the ethical environment in his business was impeccable. It was one of those moments when I could only ask, "Lord, why me?" But, then, why not me? All through our conversation, I kept debating with myself about whether I should say anything to him. Well, for better or for worse, I didn't, and as a result of my distraction, the conversation did not go well. I left his office hoping my handling of the situation in the lobby would make a difference with his two associates.

If this sounds like I am making a mountain out of a molehill, I am. But don't forget one of my theses for this book is that we need more early intervention in little infractions. If you continue building molehills on top of one another, they can become a mountain. In trying to figure out how societies (meaning, any organization) normalize misconduct, it seems that it most often happens because leaders let little misdeeds go unchallenged and they grow into bigger infractions that call for responses that are more traumatic. I've said this before but it is critical to rebuilding our moral fiber so I'll keep on saying it. I'm talking about the routine responses from leaders, such as:

> *"Everybody does it. It's not worth my time."*
> *"We've always done it. Nobody is concerned about it today."*
> *"It's not my job. Let somebody else handle it."*
> *"I can't tell everyone else what is right or wrong for them."*

I left my friend's office with the uneasy feeling, "It was not my job, but…" My *moral sense* was nagging me. Yet I knew my friend well enough to know he would never tolerate his staff representing the company, as did the receptionist and superintendent. I needed to help him reinforce company policy on smoking and to eliminate an ethical issue. But I was also aware that nobody likes a whistle blower or tattle-tale. It's not a good way to make friends. A few months later, when the urgency of the episode had receded, I did tell my friend about the incident in the context of an example of little things that can lead to greater infractions of ethical standards.

WHISTLE BLOWING

Well, what about whistle blowing? It certainly is not fun; it's uncomfortable. Tattle-tales are not popular and they generally don't like themselves afterwards. While the practice may bring about a measure of justice in one situation, it doesn't build trust. You can't build an ethics program or create an ethical environment on the expectation of whistle blowing. If whistle blowing becomes an important element, then an ethics policy or program becomes a rules-driven system simply calling for compliance, it creates distrust among employees, it and does not motivate the "high road" in people's conduct. Much has been written about this problem. What is needed is an ethics program that discourages the *motivation* toward unethical conduct to begin with (early intervention) and thereby forestalls the need for whistle blowing. It is more important to build an ethical culture in which everyone frowns upon dishonesty, and offenders come to feel like outsiders.

In the absence of such an environment, some infractions ultimately may come down to a need for action by colleagues, and if all else fails, sometimes it is necessary to let the boss know when there has been an infraction. Hopefully, this is not the ordinary situation. As I said, the ideal ethics system is the one that challenges everyone to the high road, to each person's best understanding of moral expectations, and to a conscientious effort to make righteous choices everyday. This suggests an approach by colleagues that can be helpful. What if we could create an environment in which each person felt free to talk to fellow workers, to counsel them, when rules infractions occur? Not as a matter of subjecting a fellow worker to discipline, but as a means of using the experience to talk about company expectations, about what company practice may be, and simply about the high road.

In truth, an ethics policy without penalties is as ineffective as the well-known toothless tiger. Everyone knows this. The question is: does everyone have a duty to help others through ethical failures? Isn't it better to help workers, students, colleagues, offspring, anybody avoid the penalties? Some people call it "tough love." *I call it loving your neighbors enough to keep them from harming themselves.* Candidly, I don't think we can ever reach a point where Christian precepts will restrain pathological wrong doers (the <1% group), but we might create an environment in which people feel they can counsel newcomers and anyone else (the 99%) tempted to do harm to the organization or to themselves.

This idea of the leader's duty to respond to little infractions was reinforced abruptly in an ethics workshop I was conducting a few years ago. We were talking to workers about arriving a few minutes late and/or leaving a few minutes early. The group had no doubt that the conduct was unethical and violated company policy but they were less sure that managers needed to act on such a little thing. After considerable discussion, one man who had not participated in the discussion to that point spoke up. "I wish someone had pointed out some of the little things I did wrong before I stole that car and went to jail. I might not have lost 2 years of my life." If we can keep people out of jail or keep them from losing their jobs, isn't that "loving your neighbor as yourself"?

A LITTLE PERSPECTIVE

Thomas Jefferson believed every human has a *moral sense*, the ability to discern right from wrong. Charlton Heston might say it's in our DNA. I think it is in our soul, our moral sense. One of the important ways we learn the difference between right and wrong is from the example of others. We are each part of the moral and ethical development of everyone around us and we sometimes have to appeal to each individual's **moral sense.** If we believe Jefferson, then every ethical failure becomes a development opportunity, not only for the boss, but for everyone.

There is a line from the movie, "The Confession," in which the charged murderer, played by Ben Kingsley, says, "It is not hard to do the right thing. It is hard to know the right thing. When you know, then it is hard not to do the right thing." Isn't it right to help a neighbor *know the right thing*? It is often hard to know, but, when we do, isn't it right to help our neighbor? Don't we have a moral obligation to help teach others to do the right thing by encouraging the high road but also by pointing out the incorrect way? For practically all of our social contacts, we can believe with assurance that everyone has the moral sense to do what they themselves know to be right and, if so, to learn.

Some people suggest that we need more ethical education, and we do, but this emphasis upon education will show little result if it does not speak to our *moral sense* or if we continue to ignore God as our ultimate source of right and wrong. This is the conclusion Socrates left to us, and it is the nature of Christian ethics. It does not hang on a book of law or a book of quotations from a good person. We each must pass it on to others, as Payne Stewart did. In doing so, our source of authority for rightness and wrongness is still Christ's example and teachings and we are free to approach him directly for leadership. Our friends and associates are also there to help us find God's will and to know what Jesus would do, not to develop a consensus judgment about right and wrong. Remember, our friends are not always the best source of right and wrong, even when we value their opinions, unless they help us determine Christ's example and teachings.

Whistle-blowing implies it is too late to help the wrongdoer. Loving your neighbor enough to help them avoid harm is timely and right. Even with strong positive ethics policies and practices, sometimes it is essential that followers be corrected and be led in a better direction. Nobody said it would be easy. "Everyone to whom much is given, of him much will be required" (Luke 12:48).

BE TRUE TO ONE'S SELF

Leadership is said to be a lonely business. It is. For one reason, leaders are constantly making decisions with insufficient information. You can get lots of input from others in preparation for decisions, but when it's crunch time it is the leader who is charged with decision-making responsibility. It is made even more lonely when leaders who hold to high moral standards are charged with decision-making for a group that may or may not share those standards or is addicted to consensus decision-making.

Sometimes we find that we must face our moral decisions alone in unsuspecting situations. For example, occasionally good people, trying to do the completely righteous thing, can raise ethical issues for others. I want to share an experience, not to set myself up as a shining example, but as a good illustration of the loneliness of one who holds to a different standard. I recently took on the task of starting an academic program in business in a small Bible college whose plan was to grow into a Christian university. The idea was exciting for me since I needed something to occupy my retired mind and time. The new job put me in an environment with ministers and friends who were wonderfully dedicated to a particular view of the Christian faith usually referred to as "fundamentalism," which I do not fully share.

They interpreted the Bible quite literally while I see it as God's word delivered to us and translated with many of the frailties of human understanding and communication skills. In other words, God's unique word for us was left to imperfect men to communicate. A difference in theology but, not being a theologian, it didn't bother me until I was asked to sign a Biblical Foundation Statement that asked me to commit to such statements as, "The Scriptures are infallibly and uniquely authoritative and free of error of any sort." First of all, understand that I firmly believe everyone at the school should be asked to commit to such beliefs, *if they truly believe it and if it contributes to the School's basic purpose.* It is a Bible College that, up until then, only trained ministers for pulpits in fundamentalist congregations, and such commitment to Biblical interpretations is important to that constituency. I am a staunch defender of their right and obligation to do so.

However, with my arrival, they were entering an academic study that did not depend upon such restrictive interpretations of the Bible. At least I don't think so. In fact, I suspect that the rigors of accounting might cause some students to lose their religion. Also, I'm not naïve. I know that anyone who needed a job would have signed the Statement without much argument, rationalizing that *everybody does it.* I am also fully aware that I was able to accept the position, without signing the Statement, because I did not need the job. This is why I don't want to use this experience as a shining example of my own leadership. If I had faced this decision earlier when I had to support my family, I think it would have been easier to sign the Biblical Foundation Statement. But this reinforces my point that employers need to make their moral expectations known in the beginning to employees to avoid putting applicants in compromising situations. It is part of *early intervention.* The school did that. The school was offering its program with a mission different from that of other colleges, yet they created a situation in which applicants must test their commitment to their beliefs. I was able to take my position because it wasn't much of a sacrifice had I lost the opportunity. But, had it happened earlier, I am not sure my beliefs would have withstood the challenge. Societies not only *normalize their own moral sickness,* they also gradually infect the members and as those members move from one "society" to another, the infection spreads. Too many people in normalized societies, including me, would sign without concern about the ethics of the matter. But on that occasion, I could not.

Who would have been hurt if I had signed without argument? Perhaps a student, believing that everyone at the college believed in a literal Bible, might have been undermined. The fundamental purposes for the institution would be compromised and that could mislead someone else down the road. But most of all, I would have compromised my own beliefs—a small moral failure that could lead to normalization of greater failures. Ultimately, we reached an understanding about the Biblical Foundation Statement. It would only be required of those who believed it and who were training for the ministry. Others coming to the new Christian university would acknowledge the school's position and the school's right to promote their beliefs. They would not be asked to sign the Biblical Foundation Statement, only to acknowledge its rightful existence. It was important to reach this understanding on the front end of my association with the school to avoid harm to anyone who might misunderstand my beliefs. It was a compromise but I was still left with the goal of building a business program which included serious consideration of Christian ethics. That was an important outcome and it was not compromised.

Moral leadership can't be confined to narrow structured "pigeon holes" of life. It permeates all of our interpersonal relationships. It's not only needed in the workplace, in school, and in the conduct of government, it is also crucial in everyday encounters which frequently present opportunities for leadership. We need to accept the challenge and be prepared to offer it. Perhaps this kind of leadership only calls us to do what we believe right for us, but, if so, let's do it.

SCRIPTURE SPEAKS TO LEADERS

The parable of the talents has been used to make a variety of moral points, but to me it seems to call us to accept whatever the challenge before us may be.

From Matt 25:14-30 (NIV):

Again, it will be like a man going on a journey, who called his servants and entrusted his property to them. To one he gave five talents of money, to another two talents, and to another one talent, each according to his ability. Then he went on his journey. The man who had received the five talents went at once and put his money to work and gained five more. So also, the one with the two talents gained two more. But the man who had received the one talent went off, dug a hole in the ground and hid his master's money.

After a long time the master of those servants returned and settled accounts with them. The man who had received the five talents brought the other five. "Master," he said, "you entrusted me with five talents. See, I have gained five more."

His master replied, "Well done, good and faithful servant! You have been faithful with a few things; I will put you in charge of many things. Come and share your master's happiness!"

The man with the two talents also came. "Master," he said, you entrusted me with two talents; see, I have gained two more."

His master replied, "Well done, good and faithful servant! You have been faithful with a few things; I will put you in charge of many things. Come and share your master's happiness!"

Then the man who had received the one talent came. "Master," he said, "I knew that you are a hard man, harvesting where you have not sown and gathering where you have not scattered seed. So I was afraid and went out and hid your talent in the ground. See, here is what belongs to you."

His master replied, "You wicked, lazy servant! So you knew that I harvest where I have not sown and gather where I have not scattered seed? Well then, you should have put my money on deposit with the bankers, so that when I returned I would have received it back with interest."

"Take the talent from him and give it to the one who has the ten talents. For everyone who has will be given more, and he will have an abundance. Whoever does not have, even what he has will be taken from him. And throw that worthless servant outside, into the darkness, where there will be weeping and gnashing of teeth."

If it is a small responsibility, we need to give it our best effort. It's not too much of a stretch to apply this moral principle to the leader who is responsible for the ethical conduct of those who follow. Take care of the little matters so they don't grow into great sores, as my friend the ex-con pointed out. Luke 16: 10-12 reads,

He who is faithful in what is least is faithful also in much; and he who is unjust in what is least is unjust also in much. Therefore, if you have not been faithful in the unrighteous mammon, who will commit to your trust their true riches? And if you

have not been faithful in what is another man's, who will give you what is your own?

When people come to work for their employer, they give the boss responsibility for a part of their lives. In this day and time, many people have come to expect much from their employer. Maybe too much, especially in contrast with what they contribute. Jesus' words give us a hint about what constitutes worthwhile work. Through his parable of the talents, he says we owe the boss our best work, which gives him a reason to pay good wages. At least this is the way an ethical organization should work.

As I said, leading people along the "high road" and gently pointing out little ethical infractions, which can lead to greater wrongs, is one of the best ways of "loving your neighbor as yourself." It is as much a part of the Christian duty as feeding the poor, providing jobs and housing, or forgiving those who have wronged us. We have long acknowledged these latter Christian duties, but seldom do we think about our duty to keep our brothers and sisters from harming themselves. Cain asked the question for all time, "Am I my brother's keeper?" The eternal answer has been and is, "Yes, you are to love everyone as a brother whom you love as much as yourself.

Edmund Burke, the 18th century Irish/English philosopher and statesman, whose thinking influenced the shapers of our Constitution knew this, which caused him to say, "The only thing necessary for the triumph of evil is for good people to do nothing." Is this any different from Jesus' parable about the talents? Do you question the need for moral education at home, at church, and, yes, even in school, including public schools? If so, think deeply about the consequences of not teaching young people, employees, and everyone about the moral aspects of life. We are putting enormous freedom in their hands that can only lead to irresponsibility.

Years later Albert Einstein echoed Burke's idea: "The world is a dangerous place to live, not because of the people who are evil, but because of the people who don't do anything about it." The "people who don't do anything about it" are those who purport to lead, even for a crucial moment, but all too often fall back on their *passive (do nothing) self-interest:*

"Everybody does it."
"We've always done it."
"It's not my job."
"I can't tell everyone else what is right or wrong for them."

These leadership *passive self-interest* tendencies are important because so many of the ethical infractions and/or legal offenses of the corporate world are not committed by crooks but by well-meaning, but negligent, managers. Good people do bad things, especially if we allow misconduct to become habitual in an organization.

By the way, normalizing conduct doesn't have to lead to sickness. It can also mean setting good moral habits early and thereby establishing a pattern for life. This is what good leaders, parents, teachers, and managers would like to achieve; change moral sickness to good lifetime moral habits. In Proverbs 4: 5-9 (NKJV) we are told the result of teaching followers how to normalize conduct that leads to a better life:

> Get wisdom, get understanding: forget it not; neither decline from the words of my mouth. Forsake her not, and she shall preserve thee: love her, and she shall keep thee. Wisdom is the principal thing; therefore get wisdom: and with all thy getting, get understanding. Exalt her, and she shall promote thee: she shall bring thee to honor, when thou dost embrace her. She shall give to thine head an ornament of grace: a crown of glory shall she deliver to thee.

The proverb is about moral wisdom, folks, which is what we are looking for. What do we do when we find unethical conduct? How does one carry out their duty to lead morally without confronting misconduct? It can't be done. We can't remove all the distasteful duties of leadership. Sometimes we must respond and it is not fun. But wouldn't it be better to establish systems, environments, and standards that challenge everyone to their best conduct? Wouldn't it be better to heed the words of my friend, the rehabilitated convict, who wished someone had led him in the right direction early when he was committing little misdeeds?

It's worth saying again. Ethics programs are more than rules. Any ethics program worth the effort puts emphasis on challenging the moral sense of everyone affected by our leadership. In any organization, it must be clear and written, it must be understood as a force in the organization, it must be formally and informally reinforced frequently, and, most of all, it must challenge everyone to make righteous choices. Perhaps, most of all, ethics programs should create an environment in which everyone wants to help their neighbor stay out of trouble. Clearly, those who lead must practice these qualities in their ethics leadership. By the way, if you propose to be a leader, it doesn't begin and end at work, at school, in the home, or in any one of our many involvements. It's a 24/7 job.

By way of summarizing, there are several generalizations for leaders who want to avoid the process that leads to normalization of ethical and moral complacency.

1. There should be an ethical emphasis that challenges each follower's *moral sense.*

2. Good leaders can't hide behind their *passive self-interest* to avoid responding to even the small ethics infractions.

3. Whistle blowers and tattle-tales may not promote the highest conduct, but neighbors helping neighbors avoid harm to themselves is an important element in promoting the high road.

4. Creating an ethical environment requires agreement on rightness and wrongness. This step is immensely easier if the group acknowledges the ultimate source of moral conduct to be God. He is the authority.

3

IT'S THE ECONOMY STUPID!

So said James Carville to the Clinton campaign staff in 1991-92 and so it is today. In recent years, this intemperate statement has become a coarse way of getting the attention of elected officials at every level of government (and all the rest of us). Politicians have surely gotten the message that they can argue about Medicare insurance, defense spending, homeland security, welfare, campaign finance reform, corruption in government, financial market fraud, ethics in government and anything else they believe might get votes, but don't ever let the economy lapse into a recession. Don't do anything that will throw water on the red hot economic bonfire.

WE HAVE AN ECONOMIC DEPENDENCY

No action taken by the President or Congress is to cause a downturn in any component of the economy. The government is expected to create jobs even for people who don't have the education, training, or experience to hold a job. We've already seen that even terrorist attacks must be handled in ways that don't cause economic slowdowns. We've heard telemarketers argue against "donotcall.gov" because it will slow down their sales, put their employees out of work, and slow down the economy. NAFTA is good or bad depending on whether or not your business has to compete with overseas products or whether or not you can find a job. Most of the criteria of progress in opportunities for minorities are measured and argued at the national level in terms of economic progress. Effects on our economic well-being override all other considerations in our personal maze of systems.

It will sound unbelievable to the baby-boomers and generation X, but there was time when we didn't think government was supposed to bail us out of recessions or depressions. It's true, I promise! Alas, that idea is only a distant memory. Government and the nebulous economy is about the only marriage in this day and time in which we have any assurance it will last. It's a marriage made in heaven. Wrong! It's more like hell.

It's been a long time since Economics 201 but I do remember the economy to mean that nebulous system of relationships that:

* influences the physical distribution of goods and services,

* determines who gets which goods and services, and

* arbitrates prices.

(Actually, they are all the same.)

This concept of the economy seems archaic today and it does date back many years, long before the Great Depression of the 1930's. It sounds like a system that is in the care of the private sector—business and consumers. Guess what! It was! Today, however, the economy is the system used by government, including the Federal Reserve, to regulate income flows and expenditures. Taxes once were the means of financing government but now it has a greatly expanded role as a tool of economic policy for regulating business and personal income. Government has come a long way since the "good ole days" when its role was to maintain law and order and carry out foreign policy. Honest, I am not dreaming all this up!

Today, going into the 21st Century, government is the major economic player. To illustrate, our Gross Domestic Product in 2002 was estimated at $10.5 trillion with 26% being spent by federal (incl. military), state, local governments. Our labor force was about 140.0 million, about 50% of the population, with 28% of us working for federal (incl. military), state, or local governments and government contractors and suppliers. We have become totally dependent on an economy dominated and controlled by government. Hey, don't form your opinion about my sanity too quickly. I absolutely understand and agree that we have made enormous progress in quality of life, lifestyle, income, and economic power. Nevertheless, I still frequently wonder if the economy was really intended to become the driving institution in our lives. It's a question worth a little thought, even if it is academic (and probably, heretical) at this point.

I guess it depends on how far back we look. When the Jamestown settlers were struggling for survival during their first winter, they traded by bartering at its most basic level. It was the basis of their economy but I don't think fluctuation in interest rates in London was ever on their minds. They were more concerned about where the next meal would come from. It was physical survival. If the town bureaucrat had suggested to John Smith and friends, "We need to lower interest rates," he would have been used as trade goods with the Indians. It's a different world today.

We have come to assess the economy in extremely sensitive terms as mundane as what Alan Greenspan is saying in his dinner conversation. That man can change my lifestyle pretty quickly so I no longer have the luxury of ignoring him or the action taken by Congress and the President. These institutions not only influence the economy, in doing so, they also affect social and moral attitudes. My wealth is directly affected by the government's policy to create money or to constrict the money supply. It has much less to do with how hard I work. Isn't that *wealth without work?* Shame on me!

But only the affluent can be philosophical (or flippant) about it and I'm neither affluent nor philosophical (maybe a little flip). However, people on the edge of poverty can become highly animated about the way their daily bread is affected by government. We do have too many people below the poverty line, but the number changes with the economic decisions made in Washington. In fact, the number of people in poverty is one of the basic economic measurements and the number changes as price levels rise or fall. We have become less concerned about hungry people than about the statistic.

Let me illustrate. Starting in Reagan's administration, many people began moaning about the widening gap between household incomes of the rich and poor. It did indeed widen, and Congress was pressured to "do something," meaning find a way to restrict wealthy Americans' income. Ask the single-parent mom about Greenspan's statistical comments to Congress. You wouldn't get much interest, but you would get an impassioned charge that somebody needs to do something. Nobody wanted to look at the root cause, which was the burgeoning number of single-parent households trying to survive on one income. These households were growing because divorce rates were growing; so was the number of unwed mothers, along with the number of irresponsible husbands and boyfriends. The issue, posed to Congress, was never to resolve these social and moral issues, it was always to limit income to the wealthy and subsidize the poor. Even at this late date, I'm still not sure what the church's position was during this period. The church had a lot it could have said but it didn't.

ECONOMICS AND US MERE MORTALS

Although we are mostly concerned here with the moral aspect of the economy, we might benefit from revisiting the history of economic systems. We have come a long way from the days when we could walk away if we didn't like what government was doing. Young men can't go west anymore with hopes of advancing their careers. Strong population growth is straining our natural resources. Our vision for economic progress has turned toward Washington. We wait anxiously for shifts in the economic policy of every new administration. I can remember when people didn't even think we should have an economic policy. After all, capitalism is supposed to be a laissez faire economy. I'm not sure, but that statement may be un-American today.

All this has to sound like heresy to modern day economists. Nevertheless, in order to deal with morality and ethics of economic activity, it seems that we need to take a quick, even if superficial, look at the evolution of economics. If economics professors get to heaven, I hope those who taught me will look down and have a little compassion. I take some solace with the belief that most of them will have had their own problems with St. Peter.

What has all this to do with societies normalizing moral sickness? A great deal, both in the world of foreign policy and in our personal lives. Economics, or the pursuit of economic security, has been an obsession in our world of "haves" and "have nots." Rightfully so, because we are talking about our ability to survive, to prosper, and to take care of our families. But, before looking at the personal side of economics, let me digress somewhat into the world of foreign policy and international relations.

• The conflict between capitalism and socialism was behind Germany's drive to get out from under the poverty left from WWI and it allowed Adolph Hitler's tormented mind to fester and emerge from the swamps of depression. I referred earlier to this movement in Germany. Rather than demanding reparations from Germany, what if the Allies had spent money helping Germany recover from WWI? That's a liberal idea which unnerves me a little, but, in naïve retrospect, maybe Germans would not have bought Hitler's insane leadership if we had been more benevolent. Don't count on it, but it is something to think about. Hindsight makes for interesting conversation and in this instance that's about all except for the point that economic depravity in Germany made Hitler palatable.

- Different economic philosophies spawned the split in China after WWII between Nationalists and Communists. Nationalists looked to the Allies for aid to build an entrepreneurial economy while the Communists wanted to control people's lives (and minds) believing Chinese peasants incapable of making sound choices.

- The cold war festered for so long because of a conflict between two different ideologies regarding people's ability to manage their own economic activities. But nobody thought about philosophy in those days. Each side saw the threat of nuclear annihilation as a far more pragmatic issue.

- Of course, the bad experience of Vietnam still lingers in our minds and souls. North Vietnam looked to socialism/communism for its economic development with the USSR helping it while South Vietnam, under US urging, pursued a capitalist solution. We failed in our military efforts to maintain democracy and free enterprise in South Vietnam but ironically, since the war, all of Vietnam has moved rapidly toward a capitalist economy. What a price to pay for something that would have happened anyway!

We have fought many wars when economics was at the root of the divisiveness. More than we like to admit. War is never moral in spite of the claims of leaders from Alexander the Great to President George W. Bush. Don't get excited, I voted for both Bush's and would do it again. (I didn't vote for Alexander the Great.) But even good leaders aren't always right. I thought former President Carter (whom I did not vote for) had it right in his acceptance speech for the Nobel Peace Prize in 2002. He put war in perspective when he said, *War may be the lesser of the evils available to us, but it is still an evil.* (paraphrased) Let's not be naïve about war. All too often, they have been about economic differences between nations or at least between national leaders.

I said this venture into international affairs was a digression but, in fact, it highlights the intense feelings we have about economic relationships and policies that now affect us personally. When it happens, we are prey to leaders who will use our economic obsession to justify economic sanctions, war, blockades, and other forms of action. If we are willing to sacrifice human life in order to maintain economic stability and/or opportunities, unscrupulous or even unsuspecting leaders are able to use us for their own purposes. I am talking about the stark contrast that can develop between the "haves" and "have nots." *War is a massive ethical failure* of national leaders who cannot find a moral solution to an international problem. And, most often, it has to do with economics.

I don't have the omniscience to look into the future and see a time when we can avoid wars. Even Christ himself told us to expect wars (not necessarily to condone them). He knew his people well. However, if we could occasionally look beyond short-term divisive issues, think beyond the ultimate extension of little differences, which threaten the outbreak of war, work to narrow economic gaps around the world, and do all this early enough, there might evolve solutions before the road to war becomes the normal solution. This seems particularly possible when economics is at the root of the differences, which is most of the time. The price of war, not only in economic terms, but also in human life, has magnified enormously today. Perhaps if we could persuade political leaders to change their vision a little, then, perhaps, we could help them avoid wars. War is a moral failure that illustrates the adage;—*Every society normalizes its own moral sickness.*

I can't leave this topic on such a grand but naïve note. I don't really think people, God's creatures with a full set of self-interests, are capable of avoiding wars. Sure, this sounds cynical, but it is also honest. As I said, Jesus himself acknowledged this limitation to our moral sense when he said "there will be wars and rumors of wars." He wasn't establishing a principle or even condoning war, only acknowledging reality among imperfect humans. Even so, he does hold out a better life to those who resist the human temptations to violence and who don't retaliate because "everybody else does it."

I have ventured into the world of foreign policy and international relations only to make the point that economics has been at the root of most national differences. Now what are the economic philosophies that have had so much to do with our warlike relationships? Let me leave these economic ideologies and come down to the more pressing struggle each day to make ends meet. To do this, a little economic history seems to be in order to understand that the economic struggle around the world is not the same for everybody.

Enough said about war. Robert Ruark's novel, *Something of Value* (1955), about the Mau Mau period in Kenya, was based upon an old African (Basuto) adage, *If a man does away with his traditional way of living and throws away his good customs, he had better first make certain that he has something of value to replace them.* The British didn't do this. No one would argue that the United States or any industrialized country is in for such a bloody revolution. But we have gradually taken *something of value* out of our society—our moral heritage. I don't see much that has replaced it and, without it, I am concerned more about a quiet economic revolution that eats at our soul.

A LITTLE ECONOMIC HISTORY NEVER HURTS (WELL, NOT MUCH)

If we are honest about our early history until the Renaissance period, Christianity, not government, was the *big brother* of capitalism. It was still a controlling force when Adam Smith published *The…Wealth of Nations* in Britain, in 1776, the same year American colonists rebelled. Before all the historians and economists take me to task, I know quite well that both Christianity and capitalism pre-date 1776. Nevertheless, the cornerstone for economic freedom, for religious freedom, along with all our freedoms, was put in place in the United States' Constitution. The framers of the Constitution knew the rebellious colonists to be strong-willed people on an intense search for freedom in all facets of their lives, but the freedom to pursue their livelihood was foremost. They didn't try to suppress this drive for self-sufficiency; they devised a unique form of government that encouraged each participant to pursue his/her own self-interest. The result has been the massive explosion in economic activity and wealth that we now enjoy. But none of these leaders of the rebellious colonies believed this great economic opportunity would function without the guidance of a church with clout—spiritual influence in people's lives.

Ironically, Christianity has grown with the nation, and with the Gross National Product, but has not fared as well as our economic progress, at least not in the late 20th century. The early concurrent growth by our two great institutions, business and the church, was not coincidental. Adam Smith, the Scottish moral philosopher, preacher, and professor of the late 18th century, concluded that the best way for a society to prosper was to allow each participant the freedom to compete with a minimum of interference by government. He came to this conclusion in England which was dominated by the Church of England. Smith could not conceive of a society without a strong church influence. A far cry from our day! In 1776 Europe, people were restrained more by church doctrine than by the law. Or perhaps it is more accurate to say that the law itself was influenced greatly by church doctrine.

Law was usually too remote on our American frontier but people tended to carry their faith with them as they moved west. Or perhaps it is better to say religion and the law scratched each other's back. The practice of law on the frontier was mostly an application of their adaptation of moral law, not statutory or precedence law from Europe. English law was a restraint in people's lives in the East, but often it was used by the Church as their punitive agency, as it had been in

Europe. Back in England, it is not conceivable that Adam Smith could envision a world in which there was not a dominant moral agency—the church. As a moral philosopher, he was of the school of meta-ethicists, including other philosopher/ministers as Samuel Butler, who acknowledged God as the source of moral values. His economic principles have to be viewed in this light.

As a result of the oppressive church dominance in England in the 18th Century, business in the new colonies acknowledged the church teachings on ethical conduct but gradually extracted itself from the influence of the church as the country expanded westward. For at least the first 100 years of our history, entrepreneurs, pioneers and settlers located in isolated regions; and became less concerned about anemic law or government control. Not so with their close feelings about church precepts. Strong-willed itinerant preachers coupled with a deep attachment of the people to their moral backgrounds gave the local colonial congregations an influential position in most communities.

By 1890, as we began to come together in cities, leaders of government gradually imposed ordinances and laws on the rapidly industrializing country. It was a necessary shift to enable people to live together, cooperate with one another, and create economic progress for the most people. It was the beginning of compromise between government restraints and rugged individualism that has not ended even today. The growing complaints of business only served to slow, not stop, the inevitable march of federal controls. Even so, during the whole period of the 20th century, the country prospered to a degree not known in history. Ironically, while business entrepreneurs railed against government control most of them were quick to take advantage of laws that enhanced their ability to compete. Entrepreneurs talked about free enterprise, but often relied upon socialistic government control legislation in their own businesses. Objectionable government control gradually became the *normal* way of life even for hard-nosed business owners.

The improved quality of life was not lost on consumers either. The consuming public has also had it both ways. On one hand, there was an aggressive business sector providing more and better goods, while legislation and executive orders from government intended to protect the consuming public grew at a geometric rate. Consumers have seen both trends to be in their best interest. All the time government was tightening its hold on business, consumers (the public) were saying, "right on," and feeling more and more confident as they earned and spent more money.

Until the late 20th Century, there was little concern by consumers that their own lifestyle might be constricted by too much government. Certainly, no one believed business executives, sports figures, entertainment celebrities, and promoters would become so greedy, flaunt the law, not just economic principles, and almost destroy the golden goose. All the while elected government officials became more keenly aware that their jobs depended on voters who were excited about the great opportunities our economy offered and who were also quite willing to "sell" their votes to keep government influence going. More and more self-serving elected officials pandered our economic drive. The world of greed in corporate offices and the halls of government became *normal.*

WE HAVE SEEN THE ENEMY AND HE IS US

So, the battle for our self-interest between business with its enormous list of products and services has been joined for a long time (We've always done it). And the once powerful church has become weaker and weaker. The self-interest of the consuming public has been the battleground, or the football, depending upon how debilitated you see society these days, but it has been a fun-packed trip. We have seen lots of unethical and illegal conduct in the news but, "Oh, well." We enjoyed the economic ride—until the massive scandals in corporate America of 2001 scared Americans out of their complacency. It's about time! But, you know, I've not heard anyone offer to give up their quality of life to slowdown the hanky-panky in government or businesses. We want the government to do something, but don't mess with our quality of life—"*It's the Economy, Stupid.*" Our economic *system* has a strangle hold on us and it is hard to find leaders with the strength of character to address the issue.

Perhaps you might have seen shadows on the horizon as early as Watergate, or earlier, when we saw clearly that the institution that we expected to protect our freedoms was itself capable of skullduggery. But before you begin to feel like a victim (and apply for federal aid or sue somebody!), get the battle in perspective. We are still free to buy what we want and we are still free to elect who we want (well, almost). We have prospered greatly and, as long as our prosperity has not been threatened, ethical conduct of leaders was somebody else's problem. After all, we can't tell everybody what is right or wrong for them. Wow! How many times have I heard that?

Then there is the fatalistic attitude that our opinion isn't relevant either in the board room or in Washington. Why bother voting or why worry about crooked executives? We haven't tried hard enough to influence unethical conduct of our leaders. Pogo was right: "We have met the enemy and he is us." It wasn't in our best interest. It was somebody else's job. Or even worse, everybody else did it (lied, cheated, and stole). So who is responsible?

The church, during the same period leading into the 21st century, has seemed at a loss to influence managers of enormous corporations or government officials, at least not in the process of managing complex organizations. Religion has been reduced to a Sunday morning "feel good" experience or to the role of one more welfare agency. Don't misunderstand. Even though both roles are totally worthwhile, even essential, there is so much more to the church's mission.

Today's news-making crooks have grown up in an environment in which too many bosses looked the other way, unless a business objective was threatened. Now these middle managers from the technostructure of industry in the 1950's, 1960's, and 1970's have grown into top management and have the opportunities for larger unethical and illegal mischief. They were conditioned as they progressed up the ladder. And it all seemed so "right." Now we are hearing about them on the six o'clock news; people who, under normal conditions, would not be known to the American TV viewers. *We normalized a moral sickness in executive offices and government throughout our economy-driven society.* Again, who is responsible in a nation of economic, political, and religious freedom? "We have seen the enemy and he is us."

4

AND THEN THERE WAS ONE (Economic System, that is)

It is not my intent to hold something as nebulous as an economic system to be the cause of the moral decay around us. I am saying that present day economic policies and systems do create a nurturing, even enabling, environment in which unscrupulous, self-interested politicians and business executives can use our obsession with economic progress (or stability) to do mischief.

Economics to most of us is a highly practical matter of keeping bread on the table. But behind the practical interpretations, there have been three philosophical concepts of "the economy" with considerable blending among them all.

- I—The classical capitalist supply and demand economics as first described by Adam Smith (1723-90) in his monumental work, *An Inquiry into the Nature and Causes of the Wealth of Nations,* 1776, and critiqued and refined by such philosophers as John Stuart Mills, Thomas Malthus, and many others.

- II—Then there is the 19th century socialist economics of Karl Marx (1818-1883) in which he proposed government control as an alternative to capitalism in his book, *Das Capital, Vol. I.,* published in 1867.

- III—In the mid 1930's, the economics of government intervention (not control) was described by Lord John Maynard Keynes (1883-1946), in his important book, *The General Theory of Employment, Interest, and Money,* 1936. His theory of intervention in economic activity was the subject of a letter to FDR in the mid-1930's, as a means of breaking the hold of the Great Depression.

Each of these three schools of economic thought assumes different philosophies about;

—*What constitutes a good life?*

—How people pursue their livelihood?

—What motivates humans in their daily decisions?

—How do they put their self-interests in context with the rights and desires of all others?

—Why are we here?

They are the questions Socrates asked 2700 years ago. They are moral issues that have been hugely influenced by the evolution of economic systems into our present government-influenced economy. We need to go into the future with our eyes wide open to the world of economics.

Believe me, I know that the pursuit of economic progress is not at all philosophical as we go about our workaday life. Even so, sometimes we need to understand the philosophy in order to understand why we do things as we do. I wish I had understood this when I was in college. It would have removed some of the dryness from the economic courses I took.

I—CLASSICAL CAPITALISTS' DEMAND AND SUPPLY

It was Adam Smith's contention, as a moral philosopher in England and Scotland in 1776, that a society would maximize its prosperity if it allowed each person (each economic participant) to pursue his/her self interest. Smith described a society in which, to the fullest extent possible, "informed buyers could do business with informed sellers at arm's length" in a process, that economists call pure competition. He was not unmindful that buyers and sellers do not always possess the same amount of power in the marketplace. Competition is not always pure. In fact, it never is. Realizing this, Smith also acknowledged that government on occasion would have to assume a role in maintaining competitiveness. To Smith, however, the role of government was simply to maintain a level playing field. His faith was in a system that rewarded individual performance and achievement, and acknowledged people's God-given privilege to choose their own lifestyle and livelihood, but within agreed upon limits.

In this sense, Smith's philosophy of economic conduct was and is totally consistent with Biblical teachings about mankind's purpose on this planet. Consider Paul's letter to the Thessalonians which makes work and its rewards quite clear.

From 2 Thessalonians 3: 6-10 we read:

> *In the name of the Lord Jesus Christ, we command you, brothers, to keep away from every brother who is idle and does not live according to the teaching you received from us. For you know how you ought to follow our example. We were not idle when we were with you, nor did we eat anyone's food without paying for it. On the contrary, we worked night and day, laboring and toiling so that we would not be a burden to any of you. We did this, not because we do not have the right to such help, but in order to make ourselves a model for you to follow. For even when we were with you, we gave you this rule: If a man will not work, he shall not eat.*

Coincidently, this last statement by Paul was also one of the building blocks of socialism, although it got more lip service than it did practice. Unlike pure socialism, capitalism does not tell people how to earn their keep. We are free to go into the market and choose work that is best for our families and ourselves. As Christians, we are free to determine the ethical standards under which we ply our trade. Thus, freedom is not only the foundation for our political lives; it is also the basis for economic conduct as well as our religious pursuits.

Smith's vision was for a system in which everyone would be rewarded for their efforts, performance, and achievement. Paul understood this long before Smith reduced it to writing. Smith only described what he saw, he didn't invent capitalism. Work, to Paul, was a means of support as he carried out his mission and he also made it a value to be instilled in Christians long before the concept of a capitalistic economy was articulated by Adam Smith. Actually, it is a value for all other religious people.

Jeremiah prophesied that the day would come when men would not depend solely upon the law and its man-made complexities (Jeremiah 31: 33-35). He said we would have within us the ability to choose good or evil and be rewarded accordingly, depending upon the love we show for God and our fellow man. When Jesus came, he made Jeremiah's prophesy more explicit when he said the kingdom of God was to be a condition of the soul, as he told the lawyer who asked what he must do to inherit eternal life (Luke 10: 25-37). The lawyer was free to choose for himself whether or not he was to be in the kingdom of God. Consider the progression from Jeremiah, who prophesied our moral freedom, to Jesus, who made it a reality by his example, to Paul, who interpreted the change for all future Christians. Economic freedom, the privilege to pursue our own livelihood, was not left out of their promises. The work of Jeremiah in the Old Testament, Paul in the New Testament, and Adam Smith in 1776 packaged all our individual freedoms, but they also assumed a responsible moral agent, the universal church, to set the parameters.

The Christian's freedom to choose is deep rooted in our beliefs and it is unimaginable that our freedom to choose our livelihood is not embedded in the freedom explicit in Christian ethics. These two freedoms are not only intertwined, they are interdependent. We pursue our purpose in life in families, in association with friends, in school, and in the workplace. These are the laboratories for us to demonstrate our higher commandment to love God and our fellowman and our freedom to make economic choices. Yes, all this freedom also offers opportunities to the corrupt among us, to put their self interest (and it is almost always an economic interest) ahead of their fellowman and the economic system itself. Even so, a quick look at history tells us there is really no better alternative for economic or social survival. The open pursuit of economic progress offers the greatest opportunity for the church to be a moral agent, to teach people how to compete and still love their neighbors as themselves.

Adam Smith, the preacher, outlined a social system in which each participant in choosing one's own destiny would maximize the prosperity for the whole society, not just for oneself. Some people have misinterpreted Smith to mean each individual would prosper. Wrong! Smith's concept seems to me to give us a way of loving our neighbor. This makes each of us responsible for the economic system itself; to keep it free and open for everyone, our neighbors, as well as ourselves. We like to focus on economic freedom, but Adam Smith also posed a duty to be compassionate to those who, through no fault of their own, could not compete. We have not always remembered this at the right time, causing detractors of the market economy to call it impersonal and debilitating to the poor. At the risk of being overly redundant, Jesus left us with the obligation to love our neighbor as ourselves. Why doesn't building an economy that maximizes the whole nation's wealth do that? Adam Smith's concept of the economy is not only consistent with Jesus' teachings, it is also absolutely dependent upon a strong church willing to exert its influence in the market place both to nurture the poor and to restrain the wealthy. It seems important to repeat the belief that Adam Smith outlined an economic system capable of supporting the greatest number of people while assuming there would always be a strong church to guide our daily lives.

Even so, there have been other moral philosophers such as Thomas Malthus (1766-1834) who did not believe people could be honest enough or unselfish enough to allow Smith's system to work. While Malthus was also a minister, he didn't exhibit Smith's faith in the goodness of men. He could not accept Smith's idea that if people had all the necessary information to do transactions they would make wise and honest choices in pure competition. Malthus was more of a "hellfire and brimstone" preacher who believed people had to be instilled with the fear of God, (or the church, or the law!) to make them act honestly with their neighbors.

The industrial revolution in Europe, which began in the late 18th century, created so much wealth for a few in the midst of abject poverty that large numbers of people never achieved confidence in the free market system. The door was opened for what became known as socialism. It was to become an experiment in social planning which overlooked man's need to control his own destiny and his God-given right to do so.

II—SOCIALISM

Some years after Adam Smith, Karl Marx (1818-1883), who was much more of a pragmatist and pessimist, proposed a state-controlled social structure, not just an economy, which he believed necessary because of the depraved state of the human mind. His goal was:

- to plan people's lives,
- to dictate what was to be produced,
- to decide who got to work and at what jobs,
- to specify how much they were to be paid,
- to set prices for products and services,
- to decree who went to school and what they could study, and even
- to influence marriages and birth control.

Marx's great master plan was for the good of all. But the "devil was in the detail." It fell into the hands of pragmatists and evil power mongers like Lenin, Stalin, and Mao who tried but could not control people's desire for a better life. Their system depended upon controlling people's minds, and they could not do it. Classical economics is built on the realization that it can't be done, but we can allow people to live and work in a moral society (maybe) thus allowing each of us to trust the economic decisions of other moral people. However, (and it's a big "however) we are completely dependent upon a strong moral agent (the church) to make it work. The power mongers in socialism were quick to see that Marx (or adaptations of Marxism) provided a brilliant base from which to muster proletariat support for a new form of government, communism, which was essential for breeding socialistic economics. It still boggles our individualistic American mind how people could have been duped as they were. Even so, we should have spent more time trying to understand the communist's views which Joe McCarthy labeled un-American in the early 1950's. We don't have to like McCarthy or McCarthyism to understand the conflict in ideology. The small kernel of truth in his agenda did not justify the wrecked lives he caused by his concept of Americanism gone wrong. But, at the least, let's understand why socialism did not work.

In Europe, particularly in Marx's Germany and in France, where socialism first took seed, some people bought both communism and socialism, perhaps because their heritage for centuries had been dominated by the power of the monarchy and the church and because they were hungry and on the streets. One form of tyrant was no worse than another to hungry people. We have never known this condition in the United States. Many Europeans accepted Marx's dream unwittingly, giving little thought to the extent to which new socialist governments would take them. But not everyone. There are many economic historians and sociologists who think the rise of communist governments and socialism from about 1880 to 1920 had much to do with the migration of many Europeans to America during that time. It's a stretch, but, for sure, Europeans came searching for control over their own destiny, especially their economic destiny, without interference from either government or the church. I doubt that many immigrants stated a desire to run from socialism. Many of them did express fears of both the monarchy and the church. Neither did they come to form a capitalist economy. Mostly, they came looking for freedom to control their lives.

If two World Wars did not clear the economic air in Europe, the Cold War did. With the demise of the USSR, communism at the start of the 21st century is now only prominent in China, North Korea, Viet Nam, Cuba, and a few other pockets. Communism has died out because people could see the comparative affluence of market economies, and they no longer believed their leaders. Communism, as a form of political mind control, and socialism, as an economic system, have had their day. But not every tyrant is a communist. Hitler was a National Socialist. Saddam Hussein was nothing more than an absolute sadistic despot. Even so, the economic result was misery for their people.

There is more to Jesus' statement than meets the eye when he said, "Give to Caesar what is Caesar's, and to God what is God's." Yes, it does mean we have to pay our taxes. Grumble! Grumble! More importantly, by the life he lived he was also telling us he was unwilling to give his mind and soul to Rome or to the Jewish religious establishment. No one's mind or soul belongs to Caesar, to any government, or to any other person. God gave us our privilege to choose as well as a moral sense with which to evaluate choices. To turn our will, our freedom to choose, over to anyone, government or otherwise, is a debilitating way of perverting what God has given us.

IIIII—KEYNESIAN ECONOMICS

Today, students learn economics by breaking it into two components: microeconomics and macroeconomics. These terms were not in my economics textbooks because it was later that the need to acknowledge two economics systems came into our consciousness. Microeconomics is what Adam Smith and his buddies talked about, the economics of transactions between individual players in the market place. In the 1960's we decided that we ought to tell students the truth. There was another overriding system through which government assumed the role of the referee and caretaker of our economic well-being. Government assumed its privilege of using the federal budget, government financing, and government persuasiveness to change the direction of the national economy on a macro basis. Thus, macroeconomics is the process of government influencing economic affairs.

Until at least the late 19th century, early Americans were driven by the obsession for land, which became their storehouse for value (their savings). It was the symbol of wealth and a vehicle for holding wealth. The storehouse of wealth today is not land; it is the medium of exchange itself—*money*. Savings range from bank savings accounts to equity securities. Land is no longer a high priority for most of us as a storehouse of our wealth. And, in case you haven't heard, *government creates money*! It then goes on to cheapen our currency, but that's the "rest of the story." Washington giveth and Washington taketh away.

Until the 1930's most Americans accepted the idea that they were individually responsible for their own economic condition, for their livelihood, for the opportunities they were able to generate, and for their accumulation of wealth. Few people looked to government to bail them out of economic depravity and certainly not to open doors of opportunity. Really! I'm not having another sinking spell. It was the understanding of life in the United States until the late-1930's. But attitudes were changed dramatically during the Great Depression of 1929 which lingered even after 10 long years of sapping the strength of the nation. People who could not pull themselves out of poverty discovered that government, which had heretofore been their nemesis, could provide a way back to economic stability, even progress. What happened?

After 4 years in office, with widespread poverty still raging, President Franklin Roosevelt ran for a second term in 1936 with insufficient progress to show for his first four years, but he had a plan. Americans were getting restless, or perhaps it is more accurate to say, desperate. In 1935, unemployment had reached 25% of the labor force and this was 25% of hardworking breadwinners, not just individual members of a two income household. The number and proportion of two income families was dramatically smaller than it was in 2004. People were not only homeless, they were hungry and living out of soup kitchens, waiting in bread lines, and living in welfare housing when it was available. Families were breaking up as men had to leave home searching for work. Hobos roamed the country looking for food, work, and trouble.

Roosevelt had established some government programs to provide the essentials of life, and some work, but none of them seemed to break the cycle of unemployment, drop in consumer demand, disappearance of savings, reductions in industrial production, evaporation of business investment in inventory and equipment, and back to more unemployment. It was a desperate time.

I can remember suppers in 1936 when only my brother, age 10, and I, age 6, ate, while our parents watched. My father was only able to find part-time work and my mother had to find odd jobs to help out. We walked to any place we needed to go. We ate lots of pinto beans and macaroni and cheese. I didn't know what a steak was until after WWII. At Christmas in the mid-30's we dared not look for much other than stockings with fruit and nuts. To keep ourselves, grandparents, and aunts and uncles from the "poor house," we all moved into a big rented house and shared the expense.

There were two grandparents, nine aunts and uncles, plus our parents and my brother and me living in a house of seven rooms (four bedrooms). The men built two temporary rooms in the damp, poorly lighted basement. It was a big house for that day but hardly so today even for middle income families. In 1936, my brother and I thought living conditions were supposed to be that way. But as bad as it was in retrospect, we only had to go to school or play to find someone else in the same boat or worse.

In 1936, I started school in the first grade. There was no kindergarten partly because educators didn't attach much value to it, but also because there was little money for school systems to operate them, and nobody was really committed to education anyway. We were just thrown into the elementary school pond and told to swim. It wasn't a time when education at any level was given high attention as it is today. It took everyone's energy and ingenuity just to stay alive. Education is about the future and most people were too busy trying to make it to the next day. Most kids didn't even go to school past age 16. Families did nothing that would cost money essential for food tomorrow.

I didn't know it when I started the first grade but a man by the name of Lord John Maynard Keynes, British economist and one time Deputy Chancellor of the Exchequer in England, wrote a letter to President Roosevelt, describing a new role for government in such desperate times. His letter pointed out some ideas from his book, *The General Theory of Employment, Interest, and Money,* which proposed a role for government in stimulating a sagging economy. Keynes was not proposing a new and different economic system. However, he did advocate *consumer spending* as the primary stimulant to a sagging economy, rather than the time-honored *savings*. In his view, savings only kept money out of circulation, contributed to the slow or no growth of business, and added to unemployment, etc.

To Keynes, Adam Smith's idea of savings as long-term mover of the economy was an "extravagant and rhapsodical expression of the political economist's (Smiths') religion." He was correct. I've already pointed out that Smith was a Scottish preacher and moral philosopher who merely described an economic system that offered people the greatest freedom to pursue their destiny. Smith was indeed influenced by the Christian faith and by the hand of God in mankind's affairs. For an in depth study of Keynesian economics, look at the work of such noted economists as Henry Hazlitt, especially his 1959 book, *The Failure of the New Economics.*

Instead of savings, Keynes proposed to overlay an umbrella, under which the market economy would still function, but also under the influence of government. He proposed that government itself spend more than its tax revenue to assist a capitalist market economy when needed. Ah! Ha! There's the fly in the ointment. Who would decide when government assistance was needed, or for what purposes? Three guesses!

This idea of government influence in the economy is so engrained today that it's hard to imagine a time when government controls and "stimulus packages" were so radical and earthshaking. President Nixon recognized our condition when he ran for office in 1972 when he said, "We are all Keynesians now." He was referring to republicans and democrats alike, and to conservatives as well as liberals. Keynesian economics had become *normal* in Nixon's day, and it is certainly the *normal* thing to do today. But in 1936, tax revenue was still for the purpose of financing government—federal, state, and local. It is only after the decision to collect taxes, that governments discover they also need programs and projects on which to spend their money. Wow! Who would have thought that? Talk about a brave new world! And from that day, government budgets have now become the private bank account for politicians' use to get re-elected.

By the 1960's, the emphasis changed. Taxes were collected or not collected as means of influencing (manipulating) income levels. The critics of Keynesian economics call it "now" economics, meaning the over-emphasis upon consumer spending at the expense of private savings that simply solves today's problem with little or no concern for the future. This was not of concern for Keynes. Savings, in Keynes view, implied that there was something of value in the future worth deferring spending. He didn't believe that to be the case. In other words, our purpose in life only existed for the moment. Abstinence from spending, or self-denial, only impedes growth in national wealth. Self-indulgence is good! So said Keynes in the 1930's.

How do I know this? Keynes is the one who first uttered the infamous phrase, "In the long-run we are all dead." He said this as a means of countering arguments of his detractors. If all this sounds preposterous, let me tell you a bit more about the man. During the early part of the 20th century, Keynes was a member of a group that started while he was at Cambridge and who came to be known as the Bloomsbury Group. They came to be authors, artists, economists, and others who were credited with launching modernism. They were the offspring of the intellectual aristocracy of London usually indulging in outrageous counter-culture debates on philosophy, religion, sexual conduct, sociology, and any other topics promulgating a "now" attitude toward life. They continued to express their ideology in weekly discussions long after they left Cambridge as late as the 1930's. Of particular note is the fact that their group included homosexuals, wife swappers, and atheists with Keynes usually serving as their chief protagonist. Why am I so narrow-minded as to bring this up? Simply because the Group's offbeat agenda is reflected in Keynes' "now" economic position. If one was a "Bloomsburie" in the early 20th century, one was not concerned about family, social progress, or religion, at least not enough to give up one's lifestyle. If one was an atheist, eternity with God was of no concern. What was left was the here and now, as Keynes proposed in his economic theories. It was his "now" economics that qualified him for membership in the Bloomsbury Group.

Beyond this moral criticism, however, we have learned the hard way that over emphasis on consumer spending (the here and now) creates inflation which has to be paid later by consumers with higher prices. Yes, because prices and wages constantly rise, everybody achieves a higher standard of living. Our current high standards of living, enjoyed by all (including me), can be attributed in large measure to Keynesian economics. But it has also created enormous federal debt, heavy interest charges in the government's budget, bigger government that is now out of control, and high cost of production of goods and service that have driven good jobs overseas. How now do we tell people that our economic spiral must stop before we bankrupt the country?

Add to the problem of the spiral, the dependency on government spending we have created. To spend, government must have something on which to spend. Voila! We now have government programs to meet any need, or should I say any whim. It is so big now that no one can control it, much less reduce it.

My entry into the first grade was terribly important to me but, as it turned out, so was Lord Keynes' earthshaking letter. I sometimes wonder which had the more profound impact on my life—the first grade or Keynes. Ok, maybe you think I am giving Keynes too much credit (or blame, depending upon your politics). Perhaps I am a little too glib about our national economic obsession. After all, Keynes didn't invent government's role in stimulating economic activity, but he absolutely made it a political issue and gave every politician in the free world a sure-fire ticket to getting elected. He didn't propose that government control the will of the people as did Marx. Instead, Keynes wanted to *influence* broad based economic activity with government tax and spending policies to indirectly create jobs, regulate income, and enhance the ability to accumulate wealth. It sounds much nicer than socialism/communism, doesn't it?

In a nutshell, Keynes told Roosevelt that government did indeed have a duty to stimulate the economy in bad times by spending more money than it took in through tax revenues. This obviously puts money into a depleted economy, gives people money to spend, spurs business activity, encourages businesses to invest, and generally starts things rolling again. In hard times, he proposed to replace meager business investment and lower consumer spending with government deficit spending, which he made respectable by calling it government investment.

This wasn't all Keynes said in the letter or in his theory of monetary policy, but it is the part that has dominated government policy from 1936 to date. He also said that when the economy is running hot, when people have more money than there are goods and services, government should reduce spending to a level below tax receipts (or even raise taxes). This part of Keynes' advice was not given much interest until well after World War II when people did indeed have more money than businesses could absorb with new goods and services.

Many historians have suggested that a major reason for entry into WWII was to give Roosevelt something on which to spend money and, consequently, to stimulate the economy. If he had, it would have been consistent with Keynes' ideas on government influence for a sagging economy. Well, even though the concurrence of events might allow the skeptic to think this, it is nonsense. WWII, spawned by genocide, imperialism, and greed, created its own momentum and justification for our entry. The fact that solutions to Axis' imperialism and to the Great Depression happened at the same time does not mean Roosevelt launched us into the war. Did it cross his mind? There has been much written about events before and around December 7, 1941 but nothing can give us insight into FDR's mind. We can't know what he was thinking before Pearl Harbor. But the possibility is a clear illustration of how a despotic leader *might* use the insidious nature of Keynesian economics policies. Roosevelt was not a despotic leader. Yes, for government to escalate spending programs there has to be something on which to spend, but no discerning person wants it to be wars. Do they? Thinking solely in economic terms, the value of war is not different from other spending programs as long as the war is fought elsewhere, but moral people also consider the loss of human life and resources.

Now, let's look at Keynesian economic policies from the viewpoint of the recipient of federal money. It makes unearned money available to people. Sources of the money are incidental and economically unimportant, and eventually it becomes a right—*it is normalized.* Since economic stimulation is the purpose, there is less incentive for leaders of government to concern themselves about how it is to be spent. Thus, Congressmen have little motivation to resist pork barrel legislation or social welfare for the common good. Through the intervening years since 1936, congressmen have become far more alert to the economic opportunities of their legislation, but with very little sensitivity to its moral aspects. There has been little concern about the motivations we create in people below the poverty line, at least not until the late 1990s with such programs as "Welfare to Work."

In the previous chapter, I referred to business leaders who notoriously rail against government intervention while at the same time benefiting greatly from government contracts, small business loans and assistance, stimulation to consumer spending, and/or tax concessions for business investment. Even individualistic entrepreneurs, who should understand the need to compete aggressively, to win or lose by your own efforts, eventually have come to accept the stimulus to their businesses by government spending. "We are all Keynesians now." This change in the nature of entrepreneurship, perhaps more than any other shift in attitude, illustrates the depth to which we have normalized government participation in economic activity.

Every society normalizes its own moral sickness, and an enabling economic system helps the normalization process greatly. We have benefited immensely from government programs and projects: WWII, social security, unemployment benefits, post-WWII military build-up, tax concessions, TVA, NASA and the space program, education subsidies, a range of poverty programs, and thousands of other pork barrel projects. I can't list them all or the amount of money spent on them. We have gotten richer, government has gotten bigger, spending has exploded, and we have become comfortable with government's promises of security. It has been a win/win situation, until now!

We have lost many skilled jobs to other countries because it has become too expensive to produce certain goods in the US. It's called inflation when people receive money in greater proportion than what they produce. There are several reasons, all of which have to do with the high cost of doing business in the United States. Inflation, which government tries so hard to control, is the culprit. Okay, government influence on the economy has made us wealthy, but it has also made us less competitive. The moral issue is simply that we have become accustomed to wealth that is not based upon work. It is an over-emphasis upon self, now, at the expense of ensuing generations. It also quietly depletes our national resources faster than they can be replenished by nature or by hard work. Gandhi called it one of the seven deadly sins of modern society.

We all receive higher compensation, not by providing land, not by our labor, and not by providing capital, but simply by the creation of money beyond our ability to produce. In the process, we created opportunities for unscrupulous leaders to use our obsession with affluence to further their business or political careers.

Work in every society has been viewed as a moral obligation, until now. Well, maybe the Greeks were not so keen on it. Paul, in his 2nd letter to the complacent Thessalonians reminded them that they should not sit idly by waiting for the second coming of Christ. He pointed to the work that he and his disciples did to support themselves even while they ministered in Thessalonica. Then he summed up his admonition by telling them, "If a man will not work, he shall not eat." This sounds a little harsh perhaps, but it has been the social standard for a long time, even in socialist countries, as I said earlier. Work is a historic part of the morality of our lives. We have always placed high value on work to the extent that we expect reward for work only, not by unproductive activities. On one hand we are eroding some long-standing work values at the same time we now have an economy dependent on ever-increasing consumer spending. We reap what we sow.

ECONOMICS AND FAITH: JOINED AT THE HEART

When the rich man approached Jesus, he asked, "Good teacher, what must I do to inherit eternal life?" (Mark 10: 17-31) It turned out that the man had considerable wealth. Knowing this, Jesus had an excellent opportunity to tell the man that there is no good deed or good life that would earn for him eternity with God. It was free! The man went away feeling sad but it was also totally perplexing to Jesus' disciples, especially when he told them how hard it was for a wealthy person to enter the Kingdom of God. He told them, "*With men it (entry into the Kingdom of God) is impossible, but not with God, for all things are possible with God*" (Mark 10: 27).

Now for the rest of the story. All that Jesus taught us derives from two ideas: love God and love your fellow man at least as much as yourself. To test the rich man, to see if these two priorities were possible to him, "*Jesus, looking upon him, loved him, and said to him, 'You lack one thing; go, and sell all that you have, and give to the poor, and you will have treasure in heaven; and come, follow me.'*" (Mark 10:21) Behind Jesus' statement is the idea that everything we have is on loan from God already. Eternal life is given to us, *free.* What we get in return is the opportunity to do more, to invest in the future of society, by helping where we can. It's not inconsistent with Adam Smith's vision of informed sellers dealing with informed buyers. Our first means of helping others is by competing *honestly,* not stealing what is not ours, not lying, and not cheating. He believed this process increased the wealth of the greatest number of people. So do I.

Wait a minute! Maybe eternal life is not so free after all. Perhaps we might freely give up the opportunity to do mischief in exchange for God's love, but if our only goal is to entice God to give us still more wealth or status, the opportunity cost of eternity with God is enormous. This may be Jesus' purpose in telling the rich man to sell all his wealth, give to the poor, and follow him. He was telling the man the price. It doesn't sound free until we see our purpose in terms higher than economic pursuits in this life.

So we seem to be getting closer to the notion that we are to be accountable for the choices we make as we go through life. The rich man made his choice. He apparently could not give up his wealth and left a sad ending to the story. In the beginning of this book I suggested that most, if not all, of the crooked CEO's of our troubled corporations today probably believed themselves to be good people. But over many years of benefiting from dishonest business practices they gradually normalized their selfish business transactions. They are modern day examples of the "rich man." We don't know what happened to him but we believe he had a second chance somewhere. Corporate scoundrels today certainly should not get off Scot-free in our courts. But Jesus said they will have a second, third, fourth and more chances with God. They have a choice, perhaps not about their obligation to society, but at least about their eternal life.

The existence of choice in our lives is one of the most perplexing questions we ask about our humanness. Why did our Creator give us such power? It's an historic question. As an example, in the 15th century, an Italian renaissance philosopher named Giovanni Pico Della Mirandola raised the question in an oration he described between man and God. God tells man,

> *We have made you a creature of neither heaven nor of earth, neither mortal nor immortal, in order that you may, as a free and proud shaper of your own being, fashion yourself in the form you may prefer. It will be in your power to descend to the lower, brutish forms of life, but you will also be able, through your own decision, to rise again to the superior orders whose life is divine.*[1]

The failure of the church to acknowledge the freedom of individuals to make moral decisions led Martin Luther to protest with his 97 theses. He deplored the practices of bestowing indulgences on barons and kings which gave them more wealth or enabled them to extract more from the poor. Luther was talking about an economic matter. Amazing!

The existence of our extensive privilege of choice, as hard as it is to understand, is a clear fact. While all religions offer choice, Christianity makes the exercise of choice a personal matter between each of us and God without the encumbrance of a set of rigid specifically worded rules, regulations, codes, or laws. Instead of law being our sole source for right and wrong, we are able to make moral and ethical choices individually, which establishes or results in the law. In other words, we don't wait for government or the church to impose laws. We make moral choices which guide us daily and which sets social patterns that shapes civil and criminal law. But the key is the process of choosing by each person and this leads to law, not the other way around. This is not to say Christians are impervious to the law of the land. Quite the contrary, we ought to respect law more than non-believers, because we accept our roles as participants in making law, through tradition, social practices, as well as public policy.

---

1.   Mirandola, Giovanni Pico della, *Oration on the Dignity of Man,"* 1956 translation, A. Robert Caponigri, Henry Regnery Co., Chicago.

When Jesus said it was not his purpose to destroy the Jewish Law, rather he wanted to fulfill it; he went on to say fulfillment would come from followers who earnestly tried to *surpass* the law by loving their neighbor as themselves. We can't leave our ethical choices solely to blind obedience to the law. As James said in his epistle, "Therefore put away all filthiness and rank growth of wickedness and receive with meekness the *implanted word*, which is able to save your soul" (James 1: 21). We not only have a wide capability of choice, we also have the ability to call upon God to guide us with his "implanted word" through the maze of complex decisions. I think it is the same as Jefferson's *moral sense*.

◆   ◆   ◆

Supply and demand economics, coming from an 18th century moral philosopher, allows, even encourages, us to make moral choices; to exercise our *moral wisdom*. It tells us that ultimately society will prosper greatest if all participants are free to make their own choices about their resources. But it was a preacher who told us this, not an economist. It would be totally illogical to assume that he saw his system of economic freedom in a world which was not heavily influenced by the moral agent, the church. It is totally illogical today to put such a powerful system of self-interests in the hands of people who have not experienced the moral training essential to guiding the use of economic resources. But we have done exactly that! When we are led by unscrupulous or unwitting people who haven't the *moral sense* to understand their moral responsibility for the system, our system is truly in danger of failure. This much is easy to see and agree with. What is less obvious is the myriad of little failures of our Christian ethic. These are the ones that *normalize our moral sickness.*

If socialism failed because it ignored the individual's insatiable desire to be free, to choose, we have reason to be concerned. We, too, now work within an enabling economic system of unconstrained self-interest along with a federal budget that offers a license to steal. If men and women are not able to find the high road in their leaders, history may repeat itself.

5

CORPORATE AMERICA, NOT THE DISEASE, BUT A CARRIER

In Chapter IV, I made the point that the shift from pure supply and demand economics to Keynsian economics has been one of the major social/political movements nurturing (enabling) an environment for an irresponsible society intent on "wealth without work." Let's be clear. Keynesian economics itself is neither immoral (it does not deter a worthwhile life), nor is it unethical (it does not fall short of any standard of conduct). It does create, however, an environment that has conditioned us to entitlements, government dole, buy now/pay later, and bailouts. In the process, we have come to be less responsible for our economic decisions and made ourselves prey of leaders intent on their self-interest. We can only say that Keynes' government-influenced economics is one of the ideologies that has brought out the worst in too many political and industrial leaders.

A SMALL DOSE OF BUSINESS HISTORY

Even with a wealth-creating economic system and natural resources with which to capitalize on it, there was still one missing ingredient. As early as the 18th century, there were embryonic corporations. However, starting in the late 19th century, this form of business organization became a big contributor to our economic success. However, like the "wealth without work" Keynesian economic system, the corporation has contributed mightily to the nurturing environment for affluence and, regrettably, has been another instrument of the unscrupulous. We have been "blessed" with a government-prodded economic system, political leaders all too willing to abuse it, and a corporate organizational form of business that enables executives to pursue personal interests with a minimum of risk. We

61

would be ill advised to put too much confidence in the recent changes in the law to make corporate America more moral.

The corporate form of business organization was part of the social structure in Europe long before this century, even prior to the 18th century and the Industrial Revolution. But the excitement about the corporation didn't really reach a crescendo until the 19th century. When entrepreneurs in this country began to realize the enormous opportunities in the vast expanse of the American West, they were also confronted with high financial risk. It isn't true that "out of sight is out of mind," when one's wealth is what is out of sight. Entrepreneurs with great dreams were less inclined to spend their wealth when it was to be in the hands of managers located thousands of miles away with a rudimentary means of communication.

Yankee entrepreneurial ingenuity reached prominence during the rapid growth of the late 19th century. There was a need for a financial instrument to take advantage of vast growth opportunities without jeopardizing all of the entrepreneur's worldly belongings. Viola! The corporation! As I said, this financial instrument was already on the shelf. It only had to be dusted off and adapted to the widely dispersed opportunities of America's emerging industry. It wasn't even necessary to get federal approval to form a corporation, only authorization from a state.

What evolved is commonly acknowledged as an "artificial person existing only in the eyes of the law" (each state's law). As such, it could:

- Sue and be sued in state courts,

- Make contracts in its own name,

- Limit the liability of owners for corporate debts to the money they had invested in the corporation (creditors would have no claim on investor's assets),

- Exist beyond the lifespan of the owners (in other words, the shares of ownership were transferable).

This meant expanding markets into the West and around the world and exploiting our enormous natural resources offered great opportunities to entrepreneurs who only had to risk the money invested in the venture, not all their worldly goods. Contemporary skeptics are quick to point out the irresponsible nature of this instrument. It wasn't perfect and still isn't. It can be abused. Nevertheless, it was and is a lot more effective than any other instrument available to investors. It did offer opportunities to undisciplined entrepreneurs for highly irresponsible ways of doing business and, indeed, there were crooks and "robber barons" who took advantage of the corporate form of business. Nevertheless, most business historians will point out that, even with the scandalous behavior of a few people, our nation's economic development would never have reached its present state without the corporation.

Over the years the irresponsible nature of corporations has been restrained somewhat. The anti-trust laws beginning in 1890 with the Sherman Act brought the federal government into the process of trying to restrain business's attempts to control prices and markets. This initial entry was followed by other legislation such as the Clayton Act of 1914, the Federal Trade Commission Act of 1915, and a deluge of legislation that has resulted in formation of the Securities & Exchange Commission to control corporate abuses of their "artificial person" privileges. There is now a Uniform Corporate Code that has been adopted by most states, but it is still not a federally imposed code. Then, there is the Federal Reserve Bank, authorized in 1914, to regulate the money supply, the Federal Deposit Insurance Corporation to safeguard our money, Wage and Hour Laws to prevent exploitation of workers, and the Brown vs. Board of Education decision in Topeka, Kansas which launched efforts to reduce racial discrimination and prejudice throughout society. Finally, in 2002, Congress passed the Sarbanes-Oxley Act outlining standards of behavior for corporate executives and penalties for non-conformities.

The result has been to turn the federal and state governments into monitors of corporate conduct. Even the historic legal characteristics of the corporation today are challenged. Executives are no longer sheltered from prosecution for their conduct, as we have witnessed at Enron and Worldcom in 2002. Tort law is much more sensitive to executive's misbehavior. Class action lawsuits have made even the largest corporations culpable and vulnerable for their abuses of the corporate form of business organization.

Stories of the robber barons of the late 19th century are some of the worst tales one can find about powerful leaders' treatment of other humans, to say nothing about the treatment of the environment. So, the scandals of the modern era are not unique in the history of the U.S. or of other countries, but the players have changed dramatically. There are still unscrupulous entrepreneurs, but now we also have the *professional managers* who may or may not be owners. Their job is to run the business for the owners. In large publicly owned companies, professional managers work in near isolation from the owners whose interests are simply that of an investor with no interest in management, *until something goes wrong.*

What can go wrong? Well;

* Profits may fail to go up as fast as last year.

* Market share can decline.

* A financial analyst may take a less than optimistic view of the company.

* Lawsuits can be filed by irate employees, stockholders, or anyone.

* Government can intervene in business operations to assure equal opportunity, environmental protection, safety for employees, securities infractions, etc.

* Executives or employees may cause prosecution for illegal conduct and threaten the company.

As you look at this list of trouble spots, you might ask which ones you would be most concerned about as a professional manager running the business for a large impersonal group of investors. If your total professional education and experience has been focused on growth in stock price, profits, and earnings per share (and it has been!), you would be primarily watchful of the list in the order in which they are listed. If you have managed long enough, you also have come to realize that under normal conditions investor/stockholders are not going to inquire into the items on the low end of the list until they threaten their investment. But investors will react quickly to the top of the list by unloading (selling) their shares when abnormal trends develop. In doing so they drive down the stock price which reduces the value of stock options held by managers, initiates programmed sell decisions in institutional investor's portfolios, and makes the stock unpopular among financial analysts. Now we know that financial analysts and corporate executives may be in cahoots to hold the price up by artificial means. However, without these conspiracies, the job of the professional manager is safe as long as the stock price stays up and no one rocks the boat in any of the other ways listed above.

Internal management policies and practices ultimately focus on the business plan which sets growth expectations for profit, market share, and stock price. As I said earlier, these goals are not only worthwhile, they are essential, to a growing company, so no argument by me. I am a complete believer in planning in all aspects of life. But in the complex organization of large companies the ethical perspective, even if originally projected from the top, can get lost on middle managers who see their progress through the eyes of the boss (Galbraith's point). And it usually means: accomplish the business plan. Let me use the case of American Rubber Co. (disguised) to illustrate.

AMERICAN RUBBER COMPANY (A CASE STUDY)

In 1990, American Rubber Company (ARC) was a publicly owned company whose stock was traded on the NYSE. It had enjoyed an average annual growth in its stock price of 15% for 12 years, since John Devonreau had become CEO. He had installed a wide range of changes in corporate policy, systems, and management practices that had turned the company around from a stodgy plodding company generating a nominal profit each year to a dynamic growing business. Growth not only came from better management practices, but also from diversification into other rubber products. There had been a steady influx of new businesses from aggressive investment of company funds, which had enabled ARC to get more synergism from its financial resources and from its basic product line. To help finance growth, the new strategy included increasing the debt level from 10% of total capital to 25%, which increased financial risk but it was still in line with other aggressive manufacturing companies. The management staff and employees in most divisions felt good about the company's future.

One of the systems initiated by Devonreau was a capital budgeting program to improve the use of the company's financial resources when invested in new assets, products, programs, and businesses. The capital budgeting program required a minimum return on funds employed in any project, but the return varied for different classes of investment such as cost reduction projects, new methods equipment, or new product investments. The company was highly decentralized with divisions in most major rubber products and industries ranging from automobile tires to high-tech material for space exploration. Each division was considered a profit center with different profit expectations, ROI targets, and market growth objectives for its proposals for capital, because growth opportunities were not comparable among their divisions.

The Devonreau plan went one step further in that each division manager had been assigned a discount factor which applied to his/her proposals. If the manager was considered a successful manager, proposals were accepted, after evaluation, with little question or discount. On the other hand, managers who had a history of missing their targets had their expected ROI discounted, thus making them less competitive when applying for corporate capital for division expansion and improvement. This element of the plan had been approved by Devonreau and the Senior Executive Committee and given to William Browne, Vice President for Strategic Planning, to implement.

All proposals were submitted by the divisions to Browne who made the initial analysis and also applied the discounts based upon his own records of the history of each manager's proposals. Grover Key, General Manager of the Tire Division, in the most competitive industry of any division, always had his expected ROI reduced by about 25% by Browne. This was a constant source of contention between the two men, and the continuing differences tended to make it more difficult for the Tire Division to obtain needed growth funds. In the long run, this tended to slow growth in the division, suppress salaries and wages, and generally suppress morale.

Even the communities where Tire Division had plants suffered because they did not share in corporate charitable contributions as did plants in other cities with different product lines. This caused community attitudes toward ARC to turn negative and tended to exacerbate public reaction, which was already rather negative because of air and water pollution believed to come from Tire Company plants.

After this situation had continued for several years, Grover Key learned that Browne was applying the discounts to his division without Devonreau's knowledge and that he was doing it because he had lost confidence in Key himself. Key had a dilemma. If he said nothing, his division, employee compensation, and the division's communities would continue to suffer. If he protested and lost, he could lose his job. If he protested and won, Browne might be even more difficult for him to deal with. Key had always been aware of his division's highly competitive industry (more so than other divisions) which also made him uneasy that the company might see his protest as another reason to close the division down or divest it.

◆   ◆   ◆

This is a capsulated case from a business finance course used to draw students' attention to the human relations ramifications of capital budgeting policies and applications. In addition, however, there are several ethical issues to be considered.

1. There is Devonreau's failure to monitor the capital budgeting system to be sure that it was being used equitably. He should not have had to make each "discount" decision, but he should have at least known how Browne was determining

the amount of the discounts. He also should have recognized that one of his division managers was in an unfavorable position in competing for capital and in his own professional growth program. Was Devonreau's failure unethical or was it just incompetent management? It certainly is not unethical to make mistakes in judgment. But it is unethical, however, to do nothing when people depend on your leadership. Ok, you may not agree so let's not make a judgment at this point. Rather let's trace the process a little farther to understand the system failure and then ask if there was unethical conduct involved.

2. There is Browne, who was making decisions about the performance of top executives, and it should not have been his role to do so. He was not getting help from Devonreau in a highly subjective process. He could be easily accused of favoritism in his treatment of Key, even if it was not done overtly. Was he making a judgment about Key or about the division? Most students suspect favoritism but differ on whether or not it was maliciously intended. They point out that Browne's job was to present a portfolio of investment opportunities to Devonreau that would maximize the company's expected ROI and growth. In this role, he would have been obligated to take past divisional performance into consideration. However, there was also the obligation to offer safe and profitable opportunities to stakeholders of divisions, such as Tire Division, in highly competitive but stable, low-growth businesses. In addition, Browne had to keep Devonreau happy. So, Browne's handling of the Tire Division was in the company's interest as well as his self-interest, but shouldn't he have consulted with Devonreau about his concerns about Key?

3. In the end, Key was in the position of weighing his self-interest against the interest of the division and the company. He had to explain to employees why their compensation was lagging beyond other divisions. He certainly couldn't go to the community and say they were being slighted because he could not get capital funds from headquarters. Was he at fault?

On several occasions he and his division controller had stretched the expected cash flows on proposed investments as far as they felt prudent; probably a little farther than was realistic. He knew that this was why many past capital investments had not earned the expected returns originally proposed.

All this went through Key's mind as he considered the merits of confronting Browne and elevating the issue up one level to Devonreau. What would you do?

◆   ◆   ◆

Problems of managing divisions in decentralized companies remind me of the parable of the talents. In conglomerates, there are always business or operating differences between divisions that make comparisons and rewards difficult. Jesus used the parable about imperfect servants to contrast earthly rewards of ineffective believers to heavenly rewards to believers in the Kingdom of God.

However, in telling us about the Kingdom of God, it also tells us that we are stewards of whatever resources may be in our care. We don't all get to manage high-flying space age materials in dynamic markets; some of us have to sell tires. As you examine each of the three characters at ARC, you can see possibilities for unethical conduct. But there is also the company system that emphasizes profit growth without considering all implications. The Tire Division was not in a high flying technology-driven market. It is in a mature, competitive, basic consumer product market in which prices are always under constant pressure. Actually, because of situations such as this, many companies in the 1970-80's era discovered the value of a stable, albeit slow-growing, product line. Lenders and investors like stability along with high growth rates. In other words, there is value in having a product line that provides stability, even while other divisions search for and develop the high growth products.

American Rubber Company eventually revised its capital budgeting policy to recognize the value of managing a stable product line that enhances the company's ability to raise capital. The more favorable capital environment within the company gradually filtered down and created a better morale among the Tire Division's employees and communities. Even though it took Devonreau and the senior managers a few years and a few management changes to realize the problem, they eventually squared their capital budgeting system with a moral standard that allowed everyone to be recognized for what they did. It was sound business, but it was also the kind of *moral wisdom* that leads to Christian ethics. Was the revision in policy intended to square with Christian ethics? No, the subject probably never came up directly in their discussions. But when moral people go about their work with *moral wisdom,* as expected of Christians, good things happen.

American Rubber Company represents the complex level of corporate management that has emerged in the last 50 years. It is the complexity, even though well intended to support business growth and created by legal processes, that also creates the environment for unscrupulous professional managers. Even without intentional mischief, the complex system itself can contribute to unfair, unethical treatment of people. And without close scrutiny, bad habits become normalized and may even lead to misuse of resources.

NEW VALUES AND ECONOMIC NECESSITY

This kind of ethical issue is never exposed by the media. Nor is it within the awareness of many people outside corporate walls. In fact, it is so much a part of "business as usual" that it's not always discernable within corporate walls. Nevertheless, it is a good example of ethical issues spawned in a normalized environment of moral sickness that eventually can grow into news-making stories. For instance, the impact of the faulty capital budgeting system on Tire Division's communities could easily have been the brunt of news stories in those communities first, and even in some of the TV news magazines.

In their book *Reinventing the Corporation, 1985,* John Naisbitt and Patricia Aburdene make the point, *"We are living in one of those rare times in history when the two crucial elements for social change are present—new values and economic necessity."* The new values refer to the humanizing trends within corporations, the thinking that led to the idea of the corporation as a family and less of a depersonalized monolith. The idea of stakeholders in corporations would also be an example of the humanizing values Naisbitt and Aburdene saw in the future after 1985. The economic necessity came from the steadily eroding competitive position of U.S. companies in world markets and the movement of skilled jobs overseas.

Now, 20 years later, the new values have been tried with some success in improving morale within companies, but there has been little impact on the rising tide of unethical and illegal conduct in corporate America and everywhere else. This is not an indictment of Naisbitt and Aburdene because their book was not intended to do this. Others have tried to encourage the concept of corporate families as a means of motivating employees and deterring unethical conduct. They have met with varying degrees of success. What I am sure of is the need to address the deteriorating moral condition which erodes morale in any organization. Naisbitt and Aburdene had some good advice for corporate managers on matters that have clear moral implications, but they took the well-traveled road of posing directions acceptable to society. They left it for others to point out that encouraging moral conduct, living by ethical norms, and just loving one's colleague as one's self can do more for morale than anything else a manager can do.

Are all professional managers so crass that they stoop to dishonest means of assuring their future? No! I've said this several times before, but it is worth repeating because it is important not to paint all managers with the same brush. Remember, I'm still talking about my "30% group." We need to encourage those who exemplify the moral values that make for a worthwhile life. This is what Socrates taught and it is what Jesus exemplified. Yes, there are good people managing our businesses, but also some who follow their baser instincts. In addition, there are many in between who, through lack of use, have lost touch with the real source of ethical values. Through day-to-day practice coping with corporate complexity, they have come to accept the consensus values of their little corner of society. They are good people who need to re-invigorate their *moral sense* given to them by God. These will be in my "69% group" but, without leadership from the 30%, it won't happen.

To repeat, the corporation has created a highly complex environment for managers in which it frequently is difficult to see ethical implications of their actions. The job requires highly educated, skilled managers. The very purpose for the corporation was to enhance expansion of production facilities and markets, to take advantage of a growing worldwide economy, and to allow our nation to grow. All this has happened with all its glory. Developed nations have copied our corporate business form and the underdeveloped ones are trying to. We must be doing something right. Managers were educated, perhaps, indoctrinated, to grow companies to a level that was not imaginable 100 years ago. They became extraordinarily good at what they did. They became professionals with an array of tools, such as capital budgeting systems, market segmentation techniques, computer assisted production, and a list of financial instruments to do their work. Yet, sadly, any consideration of morality of their work was seen by too many professional managers as irrelevant and best left to Sunday morning.

6

PROFESSIONAL MANAGEMENT, FOR BETTER OR WORSE?

Professional managers were introduced in Chapter V, but it will help us understand the normalization of moral sickness if we examine this recent phenomenon in more depth. The history of the corporation is also the history of the professional manager—one who was educated into his/her job rather than coming up through the ranks. This is not to say that some professional managers don't come up through the ranks. When they do, however, or even when their undergraduate degrees are not in business, the usual practice is to send them to short courses, seminars, even MBA programs, and other forms of professional management training programs to learn the concepts and techniques of the profession. In one way or another, leaders in all large companies absorb the techniques and concept of the trade.

The aggressive complex world of corporations has required aggressive objective-oriented people to manage them. Managers have had to learn how to lead organizations with diverse missions in far-flung locations. They have had to motivate workers with different ethnic backgrounds and different values to high levels of performance in the impersonal environment of massive corporations.

EVOLUTION OF THE BOSS'S JOB

The idea of the professional manager has evolved with the corporation and with a burgeoning economy in all developed countries, but with the U.S. experience as the model. Managers' work has evolved from managing things (material and machines), to managing the time and attitudes of those who make things, to managing groups of widely dispersed people, to managing systems composed of groups of people. Management has emerged from the example of a lead worker to a motivator of large groups of workers in distant locations. The skills required have also evolved from those of the most skilled worker to a highly educated planner, organizer, motivator, teacher, and evaluator. This is the professional manager.

In truth, evidence of emerging management techniques can be found in ancient China and in Greece 2400 years ago. Even the story of Moses' leadership of the Hebrews leaving Egypt includes the episode in which his father-in-law, Jethro, advises him to delegate responsibilities to subordinates to help resolve disputes. Moses apparently was more of a charismatic leader than he was an administrator. Whatever he was, he could listen, which is also a nice trait for leaders, and he followed Jethro's advice. Moses introduced one of the functions of a professional manager—delegation of responsibility.

In spite of these historical anecdotes it is generally agreed that management as an activity distinct from that of labor or ownership became clearly identifiable in the early 20th century. The period in which managers as a profession emerged is not happenstance. At that moment in history, as was pointed out earlier, the potential of the American economy had become apparent, the corporation's usefulness was realized, laws enabling (and restricting) business activities were being enacted, and people's awareness of business and markets was widespread. A different kind of manager was needed.

From about 1885, scholars and management thinkers like Frederick Taylor, Frank and Lillian Gilbreth, Henry Gantt, and a host of others began to study the activities of workers in large-scale production facilities. They recognized differences in the way work was done in plants compared to the small craftsmens' shops. They advocated such things as division of labor, task specialization, time studies, incentive pay, planning distinct from doing, and management by exception. *Scientific management* had arrived. All of this focus on the worker also demanded better skilled managers but, at that point, managers still came up through the ranks. The focus was on producing the most goods at the least cost. Nevertheless, management was separated from labor for all time.

The ultimate extension of this emphasis upon scientific management and productivity was the assembly line inaugurated by Henry Ford. It revolutionized production techniques and cost control even though his techniques seem rudimentary by today's standards. The mass production capability of industrial plants today would put Henry Ford to shame. He might have built red Fords if he had had Computer Assisted Design in his plants.

Around 1930, still in search for productivity, some people began to think the emphasis upon activities of laborers (the number of widgets they could turn into gadgets) was not the entire answer. A school of thought, later to be known as the *human relations school,* developed from the work of such men as Elton Mayo, Douglas McGregor, and Abraham Maslow, who examined the manner in which workers approached their tasks. They went further and looked at their work in the context of relationships with fellow workers and bosses.

The human relations fad became so popular that managers everywhere began to look for inner meanings behind the conduct of workers instead of simply listening to what they actually said. It went to such lengths that at times workers became frustrated because the "boss was not listening to them." Workers and managers became suspicious of one another, unions gained power, and a schism developed between management and labor.

One of the defining studies of the "human relations" period was Elton Mayo's Hawthorne experiment. At Western Electric's Hawthorne plant in Chicago, Mayo isolated six workers and gave them wider latitude about how they did their task, gave them more and longer breaks, allowed them to socialize with each other, and even developed friendly associations with bosses. Everything he did caused an increase in productivity. But the surprise came when he began to take the new privileges away. Productivity continued to go up. His conclusion, which has been tested and accepted widely today, was that mere singling out for special attention was enough to make the group feel good about themselves and about their importance to Western Electric. Amazing! People wanted to feel they were important!

People and their attitudes were important to productivity. It sounds pretty quant today. We can hardly comprehend a world of work today in which managers did not understand this concept. Business management was moving away from Sigmund Freud's vision of people, which was incorporated in Theory X management. This theory is that people are lazy, poorly motivated, lacking in initiative, irresponsible, and only looking for security that comes with wages. This theory calls on managers to provide strict rules, close supervision, and reward/punishment systems.

In contrast, Douglas McGregor proposed Theory Y, which saw people as harboring a natural propensity to work. It is part of one's human desire to contribute and to be productive. His theory led him to suggest that managers needed to listen, to widen the freedom of workers to seek their own methods of working, to give them responsibility, and to reward them for results measured in broader terms than simple increase in production. There were limits, which McGregor foresaw and included in his philosophy, but, in total, he was diametrically opposed to the Freudian Theory X management style. How could two men looking at the same database be wildly divergent?

How could the Freudians and the McGregorites differ? Because they didn't look at the same data. They looked at people at different points on the motivation scale. Freud saw people at the lowest end of the worker scale. McGregor actually developed his facilitating concept of management from Maslow's hierarchy of needs, which encompasses people at all levels of the scale. The human relations school of thinkers about management, along with men like Peter Drucker, has shaped management thought since about 1950. Their work is still taught in university business schools, the incubator for today's most leaders of industry. For those who did not come up through our business schools, I assure you that I know that business schools do not turn out every executive. However, as I said before, the subject matter of business schools eventually reaches executives who read, take short courses, and observe practices around them.

Well, if two opposing theories were not enough, there was Theory Z coming from the work of Abraham Maslow. His widely applauded study identified human motivators in terms of the need that must be satisfied at various stages in one's economic and social progress. These needs are

> Self-actualization,
> Esteem,
> Love,
> Safety,
> Physiological.

These needs are listed by Maslow in a priority, which means that individuals must have the lowest level of need satisfied before he/she will be motivated by the next highest. For instance, if people are worried about where the next meal is coming from (level 5) they will be less interested in neighborhood safety (level 4). If they are scared of anthrax and hijacking (level 4), they are less willing to take vacation trips on airplanes (level 1 or 2). President George W. Bush should have taken heed.

The woods have been full of management thinkers and new fads, but one other important contributor needs to be mentioned. I have already referred to him as the inspiration for this book—Frederick Herzberg. Arriving on the scene slightly later than Maslow, after World War II, Herzberg developed a concept of *motivation hygiene*. He said that good mental hygiene was accomplished in the workplace when people have a sense of work accomplishment. Like Maslow, he recognized different types of needs through which people must be motivated

Animal Needs (hygiene factors)	Human Needs (motivators)
Supervision	Recognition
Interpersonal Relations	Work
Working Conditions	Responsibility
Salary	Advancement

Motivating people is best achieved by knowing and responding to their place on this list of needs. Another way of saying this is that the degree to which workers are rational animals, as Socrates said, depends on where they are on either Maslow's or Herzberg's scale. Herzberg conceived his motivation concepts from a study of 200 engineers and accountants in the Pittsburgh area. But, the study itself came out of ideas germinated while he had been an army lieutenant at the end of World War II in Germany. He had been part of a team who went into Germany to find out why the German people could have stood by and allowed the Nazis to carry out their genocidal atrocities. The team found what many suspected, that Germans had known early in the war what was happening in the concentration and extermination camps, but they looked the other way because they were afraid for their own lives. The few who did stand up to the Nazis ended up in concentration camps themselves or dead. Thus, it was a matter of self-preservation (Maslow's *Physiological and/or Safety*) which came first, no matter how noble their concern (Love) for the Jews might have been. Out of Herzberg's WWII experience and the Pittsburgh study, he evolved the idea that *every society normalizes its own sickness.* He proposed that this idea is just as valid in corporations where;

* Supervisors act in their self-interest to please the middle managers,

* Middle manager's future is accomplished by pleasing top managers, and

* Top managers are motivated by the goals of stockholders and their representatives.

It is a matter of self-interest, *Safety* in terms of job security, which, if left alone, normalizes moral and organizational sicknesses and overrides all else in the nurturing environment of corporations.

Another promising management concept to emerge in the last 20 years has been the concept of the *stakeholder*. It refers to any person or group who has a stake in the affairs of a particular business. The idea is that managers, and workers, have a responsibility to everyone who depends on the company, not just the boss. These might be investors, workers, customers, creditors, suppliers, contractors, government agencies, and community organizations. By bringing in the manager's duty to all these stakeholders, it broadens the horizon for the manager, reinforces the informed buyer/informed seller relationship, and lessens the manager's myopic allegiance to one stakeholder. It's a step in the right direction and a sign that there is awareness of the moral decay in corporate offices as well as the need for more competent managers.

IT'S A MESS, BUT IT'S OUR MESS

People with the God-given privilege to choose are going to make bad choices at times leading to unethical conduct and, if enough people do it often enough, bad choices become normal. Perhaps only one or a few individuals do give in to their baser instincts, but there is also the weak leader who looks the other way or who, out of ignorance, gradually adopts the baser standards of those who normalize moral sickness.

It's like the story from the French Revolution when a young army officer halts his company of men to go into a café for a glass of wine. As he looks out the window, he sees his men marching off to join the revolution. He runs out of the café shouting, "My men are in revolt and I must join them."

Today we enjoy one of the highest standards of living in the world, while at the same time we know that the system has been enhanced greatly by the scoundrels who used corporations as a shield from the law. Has it been worth the trip? Or, perhaps we should ask was there another way to make the trip to affluence without normalizing our *moral sickness?*

If we measure all progress in economic terms, the answer is no or, at least, no other means have been discovered to continue to grow economically and still maintain high ethical standards. If we look at the contribution the U.S. has made to other nations and to deprived people, we still must say our economic power has aided other nations greatly. Yet, we are not loved in many places around the globe, even by people who have benefited by our economic and educational aid. Ignoring what others may think, we are still challenged to look inward at the change that has taken place in each of us to measure our success, and it varies widely even among Christian people.

Some Americans believe, even today, that we have a national purpose to spread Christianity to the world, a God-appointed role in history. We may not be chosen directly as were the Israelites, but many people feel the baton has been passed to our nation. Maybe, but my sense is that God depends upon individuals rather than nations. When we look to our national heritage as God's gift to humanity, we are probably trying to dilute our personal responsibility by taking it to the entire nation with power to use tax revenue for social good.

Others today see Christianity as just one alternative to fill one's spiritual needs. Still others are disillusioned with Christianity and live only for the here and now. Most all surveys of religious interests tell us that the place of faith in Americans' lives has waned at an accelerating pace over the last 50 years. Actually, it is the traditional denominations that are declining in favor of non-traditional, fundamentalist and independent faiths. No matter how you might see Christianity in the scheme of things today, we must admit that the affluence of the United States has greatly enhanced the church's ability to take its message to the world. On the other hand, there is much more that can be done. Perhaps it is too much to expect, even of Christians. Nevertheless, the important issue is that we have exported our economic system and management systems without the moral undergirding that make them work.

It is not my intent to talk about global troubles, even if there is a connection between Keynesian economics, the rise of the corporations, and the emergence of professional managers. We have taught the world concepts and techniques of professional management without teaching the moral restraints on individual managers which Christians get from the example and teachings of Christ. True, the normalization of unsavory conduct by leaders throughout the trading world is of concern, but the concern needs to start with professional managers at home. Government stimulated economics and corporate life has created the environment that nurtures the normalization, but I have said this already. Okay, but before leaving this topic there is one more part to the process that needs exploration—business schools, where professional managers are trained.

THE BUSINESS SCHOOL, LEADER OR FOLLOWER?

In 1965, I started my full time academic career in a small liberal arts school after 10 years in business. They called themselves a liberal arts school even though two-thirds of the students were majoring in either education or business. I learned this in the first faculty meeting when the primary topic for discussion was whether they wanted vocational education in the curriculum. It was a bit unnerving since I had just forsaken a good career in business in search of something I really enjoyed—teaching. When Dr. John Turner, Dean for Academic Affairs, told us about the ratio of vocational to liberal arts students I was more perplexed than nervous. I quickly discovered that all the idealistic rhetoric about the liberal arts took a more realistic back seat when confronted with the crass commercialism in the market for college degrees. This reality proved to be a comfort for 35 years as I groped for the proper place of business education in universities.

After the meeting, John, a good friend for many years, told me this discussion would happen at least once every year. He was wrong. I sensed it in conversations everyday and found myself discussing it almost as often. John also made a point that has been in my mind all this time. He gave the faculty an example of one student taking a course in Koina Greek, which was considered the most liberal of the liberal arts subjects. The problem in his mind was that students in the course were always pre-ministerial majors who needed the course for graduate school. His question was why the course and the student were considered liberal arts when it was solely for professional purposes. It has been my question ever since. He helped me reach the understanding that whether a course is vocational or liberal education is determined by the student's purpose for being there. If an American Studies student takes Accounting 201 just to know something about accounting, never intending to be one, to that student it is just as much liberal education as history, literature, or botany.

Let's back up a few steps in order to see the connection between this issue and the problem of business schools as they provide the ethical training for future business leaders. It really has to do with what a well-rounded educated person is expected to know, not only with their rational brain, but with their emotive brain as well. Shouldn't we expect leaders of industry to exhibit a well-rounded educational background coming from their college experience? For most of us, the ideal answer is yes, allowing us to move on to the obvious next question. What should leaders of industry, or government, or education, or religion, or the professions study?

We certainly expect them to possess the needed skills of their professional calling, to understand the basic concepts that drive their professional activities, and to have adequate communications skills and knowledge of their culture. Good, now which courses do we demand of students to fulfill these fields of study? Then, what is the order or sequence in which courses should be taken? Why should courses in English, mathematics, and science be taken first? Is it more important for law to be taught at the graduate level? In addition, if business management is now a professional study, shouldn't it be taught at the graduate level as well? All these, and hundreds more, are the questions that perplex dedicated professors. The faculty's task of developing and teaching subjects appropriate for students as they progress through their higher education experience is one of balancing, ordering, and selecting knowledge for unsuspecting young people. By the way, professors also have to be experts (professionals) in their fields, even as they *manage* the curriculum, and they learn it in the same classrooms along side students who are to become professional managers.

The faculty, even in business schools, carries out its duties through excruciating, agonizing, painstaking, lengthy debates, often leading to severe personality clashes. Coming out of business where managers made decisions and acted, this process of collegiality caused me more anguish than I care to remember. However, I must grudgingly admit that most often the result was good; not always resulting from the immediate decision, but from a series of decisions triggered from follow-up curricula positioning.

At the liberal arts college where I started, no one ever told the business department faculty what topics to offer. Rather, discussions were always about what proportion of the four-year curriculum any major should be allotted. Generally, a major in anything was allotted about 20-25% of the total curriculum, about 8-10 courses or 24 semester hours. Required courses in History, English, political science, and other humanities or social science program, along with the physical sciences would be allotted, perhaps, 45-48 semester hours. There were also electives to complete a four year program of about 120 semester hours. When the business faculty wanted to expand its program, there were no state standards and no agreed upon traditions. We had to "duke it out" with a liberal arts faculty who didn't see business as a legitimate collegiate study to begin with.

When I moved into the world of state universities, there was a noticeable change in the attitude toward business schools. Professional programs dominate state university campuses and, during the last 50 years, business has been the most popular. In this more favorable environment, business majors typically offer about 50% of the student's course requirements. Even so, there still remains the matter of what proportion of the four-year curriculum a student should take. There were still arts and science faculty. Bless their obstinate little hearts. We had some wonderful debates over the years and, even though I was fighting for every morsel, I gradually came to a better realization of the value of a liberally educated person. Truthfully, I was always torn between this realization and the demands of the business faculty for increasing proportions of the four-year curriculum.

Professional education of any sort that replaces work to develop well-rounded members of society is not altogether good. This is why medicine and law restrict their work to the graduate level. However, engineering, the sciences, and business offer much of their professional education at the undergraduate level.

The accrediting association for business schools, the American Assembly of Collegiate Schools of Business, is recognized as one of the most demanding. It asks business schools to limit their programs to 40-60% of the total four-year program. As the business subject matter requirements have continued to rise over the years, the limit has not been on restriction of business courses, but on general education courses.

Over the years, there have been several studies of what business looks for in the graduates of business schools. The result of these studies along with the intuitive experience of business school faculty and administrators has told us that it depends upon who is recruiting from corporate America. If recent graduates return to recruit for their companies, most often they are looking for people who are experts in entry-level skills. If the recruiter is in middle management, he or she tends to emphasize people skills and ability to communicate. If we ask older, upper level executives what they need, the answer usually has been more work in history, social sciences, and communication along with a philosophical and historical understanding of business.

◆   ◆   ◆

What does all this have to do with business leader's propensity to normalize moral sicknesses? In a century in which economic growth and affluence reigned supreme, when corporations were spawned to enhance everyone's wealth, and when professional managers were needed to keep it all afloat, business schools (and all professional schools) have become overly sensitive to the perceived needs of a frenzied business society. Business schools, armed with social pressure, have pushed the curriculum envelope to the limit, trying to arm students with entry-level professional management techniques and concepts, thereby excluding courses that a liberally educated person should have taken. In the process, many people have complained about the lower quality of education in business schools. There is reason for criticism but they miss the more important point. The quality of education in business schools is no less or no better than other disciplines. The deficiency in business students' education comes from the gradual erosion of general education, which leaves them less able to understand social issues, to understand their cultural heritage, and to appreciate the importance of moral values. Later in life, this becomes a serious gap in the education of anyone who proposes to lead.

Leaders of the future need exposure to more courses in the humanities, social sciences, philosophy, and religion. OK, so I finally admit it. Without it, they tend to lose perspective on where their chosen profession fits in the scheme of all society. They don't see economics as a social study but as the basis for business. They tend to miss the awareness of their chosen profession as a means of contributing to society but as a means of scratching out a living from society. Moreover, certainly, they are never asked to look at their profession as a means of contributing to the welfare of one's neighbor. As Cotton Mather said 200 years earlier, "Business is business and religion is religion." Each has become a separate compartment of life. There is no sense that God has much to do with their professional life. The church has become merely a nice social gathering place and nothing relating to manager's work is heard and, sadly to say, the plight of the church today makes this all too true.

It has become a vicious cycle. The church has lost its contact with corporate America. Corporate America demands more highly trained professionals. Business schools accommodate them with highly skilled professional management trainees. The professionals all too often see no need for a connection with the church. And corporate America is more and more victimized by unwitting, unethical, but highly skilled professional managers. I use the word "unwitting" because I believe strongly that the corporate scoundrels we hear about in the news are not going to do us in. It is more likely to be the vast majority of professional managers who sit idly by and unwittingly let the mischief happen. Earlier I quoted both Edmund Burke and Albert Einstein on this issue. To reiterate:

Burke: *The only thing necessary for the triumph of evil is for good people to do nothing.*

Einstein: *The world is a dangerous place to live, not because of people who are evil, but because of the people who don't do anything about it.*

To many people, this discussion of the business school's curriculum will seem esoteric and remote to the ethical problems in corporate America. Taken alone it would be a futile pursuit for morality. But it is extremely relevant in the context of government pressure for normalcy in our economy, with the pressure on professional managers from the business plan and the "boss," and with the steady decline in church influence. Business schools have played their role in the moral decay of our society.

The people who manage our biggest companies (as well as the small ones) are getting neither the education nor the motivation to pursue the high road in their activities. And they won't get it through imposed ethics courses founded on consensus sources of right/wrong. Too many leaders have fallen into the trap that concerned Burke and Einstein, and they lived 200 years apart from one another. They must be looking down on us with sadness today. If managers don't bring a sense of morality to the job themselves, it is not likely to be there. This is important to curriculum planning at all levels and it is not an esoteric matter.

Since Watergate, there has been a major emphasis on bringing ethics education into the curriculum of business schools. In fact, there has been a revival of interest in character education and ethics throughout our country. The objective has been admirable but it has not changed the trend toward more and more corporate mischief. All efforts to instill ethical education into a curriculum, whether in business or in secondary education, has been based upon consensus ethics. It is well stated in every book on business ethics that whatever society will accept is ethical.

Why wouldn't this socially defined ethics be the ethical understanding of professional managers and business writers? They have come through the same professional education programs with no voice speaking differently. Why wouldn't they believe such foolishness? The church was deathly silent during this shift in ethical understanding.

If you still think I have overstated the affect of the business school curriculum on moral standards, remember that by about 1970 practically all business faculty members were educated in the same business schools where they also acquired the set of values of corporate America and professional managers. They were and are the products of the deficient curriculum they taught. The attitudes and values of the teachers were the same as the attitude and values of the managers they trained.

There is no reason why the concepts, techniques, and skills taught in business schools have to conflict with our Christian heritage. All we need to do is understand both.

In John 7:16-19, Jesus seemed to anticipate our world of professional managers when he said:

> *My teaching is not my own. It comes from him who sent me. If anyone chooses to do God's will, he will find out whether my teaching comes from God or whether I speak on my own. He who speaks on his own does so to gain honor for himself, but he who works for the honor of the one who sent him is a man of truth; there is nothing false about him. Has not Moses given you the law? Yet not one of you keeps the law. Why are you trying to kill me?*

Are we trying to kill our American civilization, our economic freedom, as well as our Christian faith? I think so, if not in a Roman arena, then through neglect by Christian leaders and ethics in our high-speed society.

7

COMPETING WITHIN THE LINES

Once, in a faculty meeting, I listened to the chair of the education department argue for the elimination of grades in favor of "Satisfactory" and "Unsatisfactory," with a clear understanding that "Unsatisfactory" only meant the student must do more work. No student was to fail. He ended his presentation with a passionate prediction that, "Our society is doomed to self-destruction if we do not eliminate the aggressive competition that has plagued society for more than 200 years!"

NAUGHTY OLD COMPETITION

Wow! 200 years? And a plague at that! How about since the beginning of time? I have always thought competition was driving our economy and society. I wanted to tell him his whole argument was itself a concept of education he was presenting to compete with traditional approaches to evaluating students' work. I didn't do it because it didn't seem that logic had much to do with the matter. All through the years in my classes, I had been teaching students how to compete. I urged my faculty to teach students to compete and, in fact, I always told new professors they would be competing for the students' time and interest. I wanted each professor to walk into class believing his class for that hour was the most important thing in his students' lives. I had never imagined that my lifelong struggle for economic progress and student's individual success was a plague!

Seriously, let's get real. The department chair was making the point that competition had been a major contributor to the decadence in our society. We frequently do go too far in competing with one another and, yes, we often go too far as we teach students to compete.

WE COMPETE BECAUSE WE STILL HAVE CHOICES

In 1962, eight years after the Supreme Court made its decision to desegregate public schools, Earl Warren, Chief Justice of that Court, made it clear that we could not exist very long if we continually waited for prodding from the law to do the right thing. Specifically, he said:

> One of the purposes of a civilized society is to produce men capable of making righteous decisions and adhering to them. To compel obedience in all areas of life would be to reduce men to automata, incapable of making their own moral decisions…If there were no sense of love in families, if there were no sense of loyalty, if friendship meant nothing, if we all, or any large proportion of us, were motivated only by avarice and greed, society would collapse almost as completely as if it lacked law…There is thus a *Law beyond the law*, as binding on those of us who cherish our institutions as the law itself, although there is no human power to enforce it. (Italics are mine.)

This was a prophetic statement from the man who led the Supreme Court to the desegregation decision in 1954, knowing that they had set us on a turbulent course. If our purpose is to produce people capable of making "righteous decisions," making choices, aren't we empowering them to compete with one another? Thus, we can expect turbulence—differences of opinion.

Because we have choice, it is what stimulates our growth: mental, physical, sociological, and moral (if we use it right). *How* we make our choices and *how* we compete, is what needs attention. Competitiveness is obvious even in the little things we do. I want my grandchildren to succeed, even excel in some sport. The two oldest are already showing signs of doing that but we also have an infant grandson, Pate. He has been showered with all the technological extravagance of toys and infant's equipment that are available today. The total investment is surely several thousand dollars. It is unbelievable what toys cost these days, but, more importantly, I want him to play ball (in whatever form he chooses), but nobody thought to give him a ball. *Normal* people know infants who can't sit up do not need a ball, yet. But I have often been accused of thinking differently (I won't say abnormally), so I think it is never too early to start. To my way of thinking, as he began to sit up, he needed a ball and I bought one for him for $1.97. That kid had to be ready to compete!

Before we buy into this non-compete philosophy, we need to be shown a better way to protect our freedom of choice, to keep our country and American civilization strong, to provide the resources to help those who cannot compete, and to leave home each morning prepared to provide for our families.

Warren's *Law beyond the law* can only be interpreted to be our Creator. It refers to the God who gave us our freedom to choose, enabling us to compete. Warren was telling us that unless we faced up to the expectations of God we would forfeit our freedom to choose to the courts. In many ways, this has happened. Our freedom to choose is God-given, not government-given, and puts us in competition with all others who also can choose. How we manage our choices is at the heart of how we will be received in the Kingdom of Heaven.

Instead of trying to take competition out of our lives, we will be better off to learn how to compete morally. Earl Warren was speaking to an audience to explain the Supreme Court's position on desegregation and the 1954 decision in Brown vs. the Board of Education in Topeka, Kansas. He, and the Court, had concluded that we must end segregation, discrimination, and prejudice. We must be able to compete as equals because it is in our genes. Even Earl Warren did not envision a society totally dependent upon government interpretation of what is moral and ethical. He pointed out clearly that we couldn't have a civilization in which moral restraints should not be "binding on those of us who cherish our institutions." He was telling us that we must learn to compete morally, and teach young people of every race how to compete morally, within the rules without waiting for the law to act. Warren's concept of the "Law beyond the law" implies that we, individually and separately, have access to a higher Law. I also believe we have that access, as did Socrates, Aristotle, Thomas Jefferson, St. Thomas Aquinas, Adam Smith, John Stuart Mills, and most other moral philosophers throughout history.

As I said, my Christian heritage tells me that the *Law beyond the law* can only refer to God, but I didn't come to this conclusion without a lifetime of questioning, studying, learning the precepts of Christianity, and soul-searching. I know just enough about the other major faiths to believe fully that they teach much the same thing with regard to how we should live together. However, I am most familiar with Christianity, so allow me to argue from that perspective.

Warren was also telling us that our future requires us to internalize the *moral wisdom* of God, make it our own, face our moral choices, and not accept blindly the laws of the Supreme Court. The fact that many people wanted to impeach Warren is a little scary today. But much earlier, people had also asked Socrates to drink hemlock, and still others had Jesus crucified, yet today we look to both of these men for moral guidance. Perhaps today, 40 years later, we can also consider the sober warning from Chief Justice Earl Warren.

BUT WE ALSO COMPETE TO SATISFY OUR PRIDE

When men who already have everything still try to beat their competitors to death, it is not just for profit, it is not simply to maintain employment for employees, and it is not only to grow the stock price. Too many executives compete solely to be the best at any price, the biggest, or the most profitable. It is to satisfy their pride.

Competing to beat the brains out of the opposition is a mission of pride, not an economic imperative of the market place. Work hard, work smart, and expect employees to do the same thing, but don't destroy competitors, markets, or the market system simply to satisfy pride. If an inefficient competitor falls by the wayside, so be it. Economically and morally speaking, we conclude that the competitor is better suited to some other calling. Is this a principle of our economic system or is it a principle of the Christian faith? Why can't it be both?

Society will reach its greatest prosperity with each economic participant pursuing his/her economic self-interest as informed buyers dealing at arms length with informed sellers. So states the philosophy, laid out by Adam Smith, and practiced by reputable businessmen and women throughout recorded history.

Remember the Biblical story of the rich man in which Jesus listened to a good man who had obeyed the Mosaic Law all his life and asked what he must do to gain eternal life. Jesus told him to sell all he had and give to the poor. The rich man went away sad. Why, because he could not live without his possessions? Maybe, but perhaps he was being asked to swallow his pride, to accept the reality that other people would be richer than he, and to reduce his status in life to an ordinary person dependent on others for his livelihood. Obsessive pride can become stumbling blocks to creativity and to a moral life.

Pride makes some people overly competitive. For these people, competition is a game, not a means of growing an economy or contributing to society. Pride offers no pleasure out of having money, or talent, or anything else, only out of having more of it than anyone else. It is the comparison with others that ignites one's pride and makes some people too competitive. It eventually leads to the conclusion that what one believes to be right is right. It makes one come to believe that they are God, not just God's creation. My "1% group" is made up of these types: people who know only their own self-interest, totally evil people who lie, cheat, steal, rape, and murder just to prove they can. With them, it is pathological. They've never learned to control their self-centered pride.

But the "30% group" also includes leaders who are pridefully competitive. These leaders have their tastes for power or wealth whetted by opportunities for competitive advantage that sometimes takes them "outside the lines." You find them in the ivory towers of business insulated from the law or any form of moral restraint. They also hole up in the depths of large organizations, in small businesses, certainly on athletic fields, among political demagogues, and among educators and administrators. And, sadly, you find them among church leaders who want their church to be the biggest or the fastest growing.

In his book, *Mere Christianity*, C. S. Lewis distinguishes among four forms of pride. He makes it clear that not all pride is evil. I agree completely! So let's try to make a distinction.

First, the pride we feel by achieving some worthy goal is not evil. It's a good thing. But it is pride in something already accomplished, and it can be used to motivate more successes. It is not immoral to feel a sense of pride in accomplishment. Just don't flaunt it.

Second, being proud of one's children or students is not bad either, as long as it is honest in the evaluation and it does not elevate the child or student in their own eyes. Neither should this type of pride cause us to say we are a great parent or teacher. It, again, should only be means of recognizing good qualities in children as a means of challenging them to do more and about whom we have warm, affectionate feelings.

Third, according to Lewis, Christians have no reason to be proud of their closeness to God or their citizenship in the Kingdom of God. After all, it was a gift. We don't earn it even if we do hold leadership positions in society. He seems to be saying there is a difference between the closeness that enables us to worship God and want to share and thinking we are closer than others to Him. We should not allow this latter kind of pride to degenerate into a "holier than thou" kind of attitude towards other people within our faith or of other faiths.

Finally, we sometimes try to defuse our pride by giving to others, sitting in church with people from all social backgrounds, by reducing ourselves to a subordinate's level to be a listener, by supporting community projects or even minority group agendas. Keep it up! But then ask yourself why you do these things. Is it because you want to help society or employees, or is it because you want to be seen as one who helps? There's a prideful difference.

So, why do we compete? Do we do it to exercise our set of choices in contrast with everyone else's choices and thereby improve our talents and skills in the process? Or, do we compete to beat the brains out of anyone who thinks they are as good as we are? Pride should be contained within ourselves, in our souls, not flaunted.

Incidentally, once competitors know we have an uncontrollable pride, they have the perfect weapon with which to defeat us. Think about it.

WE DON'T EVEN KNOW HOW TO TEACH COMPETITION

Some years ago, I was attending a workshop in which a professor was presenting his case study video to a group of us assembled to learn techniques for teaching case studies. The video was about a wholesale jewelry salesman who called on one retailer and told him that his competitor two doors away had bought certain items. He made a sale. He then went to the competitor down the street and told him the same thing in reverse, and made another sale. The professor's video was intended to illustrate sales techniques for his students in sales management classes, and it never occurred to him that he was illustrating unethical conduct. The fact that the salesman was lying never entered the professor's mind. The salesman was giving false information to his customers, thus causing them to make potentially poor choices. The salesman knew how to use his tools. He had used the pride of each storeowner against one another to make two sales.

The professor was highly offended when several of us challenged the ethics of his video. Yes, even in the hallowed halls of academia we sometimes find ourselves going too far as we teach competition in the "harsh" business arena. Sometimes, in an effort to teach the basic techniques, we forget that something can be unethical. We lost sight of right and wrong because we had normalized our academic sickness just like everybody else. The pursuit of our own disciplines reigned supreme, right or wrong.

To teach young people (and adults) to avoid competition is to take one more step toward normalizing wrong-headedness. It says avoid choice and have it all. Wrong! To encourage students not to compete is to tell them to quit choosing, to adopt the life that blows with the wind. It would say that we should let someone else dictate the direction of our lives. If you really want to destroy properly focused pride for the right purposes, this will do it.

To some people who have given up on our economy, nothing is worth the hard work of doing something better than others. This is one of the by-products of lack of pride, which also damages the competitive process in a market economy. Indeed, there are large numbers of people today who have learned to avoid competition, but they still want to have it all; a skilled job without the skills, control over their lives without the resources to do it, sex without commitment, an opinion about government and other social institutions without the insight to understand even their own opinions. Such people don't seem to realize that life without choice makes it their sole function in life to submit to someone else's set of choices. Making choices results in competition, and, yes, it can get out of hand, but not making choices will destroy such sluggards. If enough people resort to reliance on others for their decisions in life, our economy and society will be seriously damaged.

Avoiding competition also contradicts our economic freedom, our political freedom, our religious freedom, and even our freedom of social lifestyles (I add this latter freedom with some frustration.) Most of all, it means we surrender our own moral purpose to the will of others. No, elimination of competition is not the answer, even if we could do it. It's not competition that is destroying us; it is lack of attention to *the rules*! *The rules!*

Many people see the business world as the playground for unscrupulous self-centered greedy power mongers and money grabbers. If the stories in the media were our only indication, there would be good reason for their opinions. Frankly, there are too many such white collar scoundrels in leadership positions throughout our society. Even if there are crooks in the boardrooms, the solution is not to teach young people to avoid career goals to reach for the boardroom. Rather, it is to teach the *rules of competition* which have guided us in the past and which are soundly grounded in Christian ethics.

What we know about competition comes most often from media reports of its abuses. What these reports tell us is that leaders have also forgotten their duty to safeguard the competitive systems. Regrettably, it seems necessary to go back and teach *morality* to some of our politicians and corporate leaders who have grown up in our increasingly immoral society and now set the standards for young people. Now here's a task for a church groping to find its place today. Let's face reality. We have been morally lax in the last half century, and it has caught up with us. Nevertheless, I do hear a lot of talk about morality, ethics, and character as we start the 21st century. Does this suggest a chance to change? Maybe.

In a visit to China in 1989 and in 2002, I was most impressed with the new entrepreneurs on the streets, selling their wares, and competing with one another.

Boy, do they compete. In a communist controlled nation, the people's will to compete has not been suppressed. They want to choose their own lifestyle. They wanted to use the God-given abilities to survive and prosper as much as anyone else.

As I said in the beginning, this freedom to choose is not by accident. It is God-given, enabling us to choose, on our own, a moral life or not. The fundamental mission of Christianity has been to remove the legalistic definitions of rightness and wrongness and develop people capable of making moral choices themselves. We were given the example and teachings of Christ as our guide, not a set of laws, codes, conventions, or guidelines. We are to make our own determinations of "the right thing to do" and it is on our use of this enormous freedom that we will be judged.

THE BIBLE ON COMPETITION

In Matthew 20: 1-16 there is a frequently misinterpreted parable from Jesus to illustrate what the kingdom of heaven will be like. He said it will be like the vineyard owned by a landowner who hired workers at various times during the day and, at the end of the day, paid them all the same. The competitive nature of workers was evident even then since those who had started early in the morning complained that they had been cheated. It was a prideful human reaction to an economic injustice. The landowner replied that he had the right to pay people as he pleased and each had received at least a day's wage for a day's work in the custom of the day. But the workers still went away grumbling. Obviously, there was no "High Priest of Labor" back then. Clearly, we can't update this story to our day of litigious labor relations. No, the message is about the kingdom of heaven, which is a condition of the soul, not about employee relations. Nevertheless, there are several moral messages in this parable, three of which touch on the point about competition.

1. The landowner's concept of fairness was to give everyone at least what he earned. He wasn't taking money from anyone. He met the competitive rates. No one was cheated out of the going rate. So it wasn't about inadequate pay for the work. It was about the hurt pride of those who worked longest.

2. He also had compassion for those who, for whatever their reason, did not get the opportunity to work in the early morning and were still

standing, waiting for work, even in the late afternoon. Maybe the parable's message is if we, in the position of the landowner, do our best in this life, our reward will come in the form of more opportunities to do God's will.

3.   Then, maybe Jesus was telling his listeners that they needed to learn how to compete and when to "turn it off." Perhaps our ability to compete within the lines he drew for us will have something to say about our reward in the Kingdom of God.

Some say Jesus was telling us that this world is not always going to be fair, but we still must stay in the game to develop our moral sense in the school of hard knocks. It is about the nature of the kingdom of God that resides in the souls of individuals. For Christians, it is a parable about where competition ends and compassion begins. But, in order to make a contrast for his listeners, Jesus acknowledged the necessity of competing in this life. *He did not advocate the elimination of competition!* He was not condoning unfair competition or labor practices. He was just using the right to choose, which everyone understood, in order to say there would be competition and we need to learn how to deal with it as people of the Kingdom of God.

Let's consider another parable to help our perspective. Since the beginning of recorded time, there is evidence of competition in all of creation. Plants compete with each other for water and light, animals compete for space, food, and mates, and mankind competes like all other living creatures. We understand that we must "root hog or die." Thus, Jesus used another parable in Matthew 25: 14-30 about the master who, before he left on a trip, gave money to three servants to invest for him in his absence. To one he gave five talents, to a second he gave two talents, and to third he gave one talent. The first two servants went into the market, competed for their master, and increased his wealth but the third hid his one talent and returned it to his master with no profit. He seemed to be *proud* of himself because he did not compete. The two who increased the master's wealth were rewarded but not the third. He was severely reprimanded and sent away.

Jesus summarized his parable with this moral: *"For to everyone who has, more will be given and he will have in abundance; but from him who has not, even what he has will be taken away."* Strangely enough, it's again not about wealth. This is another parable intended to describe attributes of the soul in which the Kingdom of Heaven resides. Those who do the most for God's kingdom will be rewarded greatest and we need to know more about this duty. One thing is sure; the parable puts our lifelong search for a moral life into the struggle for eternity. It describes life on this earth as the place where we seek the meaning of a good life. This was Socrates' agenda, and Jesus came to illustrate that good life for us. Jesus, the profound teacher, is again using the competitive condition of life on earth to contrast with perfect life in the Kingdom of Heaven. He was telling his disciples and us that we are to receive from fruits of our labor in proportion to the way we handle our relationships with others, because this is the essence of the Kingdom of God. And just maybe, the fruits will be more responsibility to serve God. It is Christian ethics, revealed by the example and teachings of Jesus. But in the contrast of the parable, Jesus was again acknowledging that our earthly life is one of competition. We understand it, and he uses what we understand to contrast our competitive drive with a better more serene life in the Kingdom.

The two parables, the one about the landowner and his vineyard and the other about the master and the talents, have a very subtle message for us, not only about the nature of the Kingdom of Heaven, but also about the competitive "dog eat dog" workaday world we live in. It seems to tell us that our life on earth is a testing ground, or perhaps a molding process, to shape us for eternity with God. It is about how we work together as fellow laborers in God's vineyard. It calls us to compete everyday of our lives. But each parable tells us we must find a way to do it morally, i.e. doing for others as we want them to do for us. I think even Socrates would agree.

The parable, as I said in Chapter V, is about the master and the talents he left with his servants, from Matthew 25: 14-30, has always reminded me of the similarity with managing decentralized companies like American Rubber Company. In these companies, division managers are given profit responsibility and they are expected to grow their division's profits. The rewards go to the managers who grow their profits the greatest, creating enormous stress and is part of the reason why so many managers choose to opt out of the process. Maintaining last year's profit is not enough; each division must increase its contribution so the overall business can grow, keep up with inflation, and compensate the owners. It is a stressful process; it is competition, and it drives all of our economy. Often, in their stress, corporate managers do forget the *rules of competition* and some go beyond the limits of the law, not to mention the "Law beyond the law." Even so, these executives, along with our public school teachers, college professors, legislators, and everyone else, must accept competition and learn to cope with it morally. It's a fact of life. We grow or we perish. But we also have a duty to our American civilization and to God to teach young people the proper limits of competition or our American civilization will fail and our eternity will only be as far as we can see in this life.

LET'S NOT FORGET ADAM SMITH
(I WON'T LET YOU)

As I said in Chapter IV, when Smith described our economic system, he encouraged competition as the engine that drives it. For starters, he called it;

Informed Buyers dealing (competing) with *Informed Sellers*

As simple as the idea is, it's the heart of a market economy, yet, over the years, we seem to have ignored the most important word, *informed*. This word also sets the rules for competition. It assumes both parties to any transaction have sufficient information to make intelligent choices. It assumes neither party withholds information, distorts information, or abuses a position of power to complete a transaction, as did the salesman to the jewelry retailers. These are all big assumptions. In Adam Smith's day, with strong, sometimes dictatorial, church influence, moral conduct of market participants was a matter for church attention.

For instance, there was an episode in Williamsburg in the early 18th century that illustrates the power of the church to restrain businesses. Prior to the Revolution, the rector of Bruton Parish Church, a congregation of the Church of England, was also owner of the very successful mercantile store. However, the euphoria of his economic activities soon overpowered his dedication to his ministerial duties and he began charging high prices and usurious interest rates to customers who owed him money—20-30%. My, how times change our perspective. Eventually his parishioners became so mad they put him on a ship and sent him back to England. And, incidentally, there is no record of objection from any government authority. Even church fathers were expected to live by Biblical teachings, or pay the price.

But the size and power of businesses have gradually grown over the last two centuries, as corporations have become the dominant form of organization in the business world. For many years, the corporation has been viewed as a veil standing between executives and corporate stakeholders, thus creating an air of aloofness about corporate accountability. The hanky-panky in the ivory towers, which reached a crescendo about 1970, changed all that. From that point, civil and tort law began to change and today executives themselves are being held accountable for their misbehavior. But, even now, as we enter the 21st century, the law has done little to curb the propensity to do mischief. Why? Economists would say opportunities outweigh the risks.

True, but we can put it in more practical terms. Whatever else there is to business, as one of our powerful institutions, it is an integral part of all human endeavor. Its leaders are subject to the same rules of conduct that undergird all of society. Too many business executives and government officials in the U.S., as we start the 21st century, have forgotten that they do not function in a vacuum. They sometimes conclude that the law does not apply to them or it is easily evaded. There are too many layers of middle managers and lawyers between them and the law. They become insulated. But we can't send them back to England today, can we? Maybe not, but there are jails here in the colonies these days, albeit they are overflowing.

Some executives have been rudely awakened by legal and public reaction to misdeeds in recent years as disillusionment among us mere mortals has built up. Nevertheless, I still believe we have to reduce the motivation to mischief if we are to make moral progress in the executive office. And it is too late to do this after they have perpetrated their mischief. Remember, my premise is that our best plan of attack is on the little ethical misdeeds before they can grow into major criminal acts. Early intervention!

This is where the church can play an important role. It can give serious attention to everyone's moral training, including those who will lead. It can use its power of persuasion to counter the secularization of the industrial world. The moral restraint of the church as an influential factor has become invisible. Cotton Mather's statement over 200 years ago, "Business is business and religion is religion," was prophetic beyond his times. The schism between business and religion is wider today than Cotton Mather himself could have dreamed.

THE STATE OF COMPETITION IN THE 21ST CENTURY

The big concern by economists and financial analysts in the first months of this century was our stock market that fell 40% by the fall of 2002. Like all economic measurements, this observation is a mere statistic. The gut wrenching reality of the matter was that the value of family personal portfolios lost over $8.0 trillion dollars. This caused many investing families to get out of the market and put their remaining funds in more stable and secure investments, such as CD's, government bonds, corporate bonds, fixed maturity IRA's, and real estate. However, the problem dug even deeper into the lives of millions of families as their nest egg for their children's education vanished, retirees and spouses had to go back to work, spending habits reverted to leaner times, and basic financial security vanished. Even so, President George W. Bush urged Americans to keep spending. Let's show Osama Bin Laden that he can't deter our lifestyle! Well, perhaps Bin Laden could not, but a lot of greedy corporate executives and Wall Street analysts did. The stark reality is that large numbers of people have been irreparably damaged, not by Al Quada, but by corporate financial pirates.

It began in the early 1980's, as naïve investors poured money into dot com pipe dreams. These internet companies, started by young entrepreneurs who thought they had found a way to compete without profit, poured investor money into worthless ideas. By the year 2000, gullible speculators had lost over $4.0 trillion (by the early count) in about 1,000 Initial Public Offerings that no longer existed. The impact on the whole stock market was estimated greater than $8 trillion. As one friend said, "That's too many zeroes for me; I understand the $80,000 that I don't have anymore."

In this environment of financial fiasco, some of our largest companies who represent such a large portion of the U.S. economy were hit with another blow that shook confidence in our market economy. On top of the losses from the dot com fiasco, large highly respected companies have been hit by an array of illegal conduct charges aimed at their executives who had been acting in their own self-interest. Adam Smith's basic principle of competition was aborted. Buyers and sellers were left uninformed intentionally. They were duped! This is the root of my concern about the condition of the free market system in the U.S. at this point in our economic history—the golden goose lies mortally wounded. Let me remind you of a few examples that made the headlines.

Enron (a Texas electric power utility) overextended its credit capacity by making use of "off-balance sheet financing" for projects totally unrelated to their core business of providing electric power. Enron executives did this by setting up separate corporations, partnerships, and joint ventures to undertake ventures in which they saw opportunities. This allowed them to avoid reporting their financial activities to their stockholders, creditors, and others, but only with their auditors "looking the other way." Enron made over 4,000 such financing arrangements without the means of covering their off-balance sheet obligations. They are now, in 2004, feverishly trying to restructure the company's core business to remain afloat and to keep customers from loss of electric power.

Government agencies do this with different instruments. To keep capital expenditures out of capital budgets, agencies will enter into operating leases or write several purchase orders for parts of automobiles rather than one order for the whole car. If it is a big deal, they may get caught and charged with criminal conduct. Wouldn't it be better to discourage the practice when small expenditures are in question?

Arthur Andersen, the Enron auditors and consultants, and one of the most reputable accounting firms in the nation for 90 years, was found to be involved in the fraud because they knew of the scam and participated in it. Andersen advised Enron executives how to handle certain illegal and unethical transactions, and Andersen accountants destroyed records that would have proven Enron executives' fraud, as well as their own. By 2002, the largest accounting/consulting firm in the United States no longer existed. Their employees dropped from 28,000 worldwide to less than 2,000 in a matter of weeks, and those remaining were primarily working to close out the company.

Worldcom (one of the largest telecommunications firms in the world) expanded its business and overstated its growth by violating one of the most basic accounting principles. If you have taken an accounting course, you can easily understand the blatant fraud perpetrated by Worldcom. It is fundamental, even in Accounting 201, that companies clearly distinguish between expenses and capital expenditures. We do this because expenses only benefit the year in which they are incurred, but expenditures for capital investment are to benefit future years and contribute to growth. So we separate these investment costs in order for them to be distributed to the future years of their use. Over a period of 5 years Worldcom classified, as last reported, about $9.0 billion of expenses as investments in capital assets. This allowed them to present to investors, banks, and others Income Statements that overstated profits by $9.0 billion (at last report) and Balance Sheets showing $9.0 billion in capital assets that did not exist and which were not available for future growth as investors expected.

Executives of Tyco, one of our major manufacturing firms, were found guilty of "insider trading" in their stock. The company's Chairman was found guilty of misusing about $600 million of company money as well as failing to pay sales taxes on certain purchases of artwork. He and his executives were also found guilty of improper accounting practices on reports to stockholders and the financial community. At the time of this book's writing, the chairman was facing indictment for these shenanigans. Tyco's stock price fell to about 25% of its value and their stockholders took large losses. Ultimately, all of their top executives were replaced.

—ImClone (a medical products company) had its application to market a major drug product denied by the federal government's Food and Drug Administration. The ruling was a surprise to company officials because they fully expected approval. When the CEO learned that approval was going to be denied he told his family members and some friends so they would be able to sell their stock before the price fell. The CEO, and others, violated the Securities & Exchange Commission's insider trading laws. He admitted his guilt and went to prison while members of his family and some prominent friends (Martha Stewart) were investigated for their role in violating "insider trading" laws.

All these cases and others were ongoing at the time of this writing, so details will have changed. But, these and too many other reports of misconduct have exposed some of our very best corporations for improper accounting practices and for publishing misleading information to misstate financial disclosures. But the worst of it is that these misrepresentations have been practiced for decades, creating need for reform of reporting laws. Our competitive system has taken a serious blow.

By 2002, it was difficult for readers of annual reports and 10-K reports to the SEC to know what the true worth of their company was. Thus, investors lost confidence in the financial markets that had functioned on trust for over a century. The stock market euphoria ended, the bubble burst, naïve investors were crushed, and many solid investors suffered because the mass rush to wealth by uninitiated investors was just a pipe dream.

In a democracy, you can stimulate government action by getting elected legislators to believe there are enough upset voters to jeopardize their re-election. We are still a democracy, but sometimes legislators act without full information solely to appease voters. This may be the biggest euphemism I resort to in this book. Our legislators always have "knee jerk" reactions to issues that threaten voting patterns. The relevance of the system in 2002 was that the US Congress passed legislation to improve reporting by corporations to their stockholders and to government agencies. It called for accountability of CEO's for their financial statements and harsh penalties on auditors, among other things.

These events and concerns by the investing public have caused the most severe drop in stock prices since the Great Depression of 1929. Investors, employees, creditors, and other stakeholders are now living in fear that their company will be found guilty of some crime and their investments or stake will be severely damaged. They are scared and rightfully so because they have had to stand helplessly on the sidelines and watch a lifetime's savings go out the window. When will we learn that when hucksters tell us the returns will be unbelievable, they surely will be? Today in the U.S., people's immediate reaction to such scares, even from their own foolish investments, was to turn to the government for a remedy. But it hasn't worked.

WHAT IS A SOCIETY TO DO?

Well, if the law will not restrain people who would do mischief in the market-place, who or what will? Let's get really basic for a moment. We are talking about the capitalist economic system that emphasizes freedom for every participant to pursue his/her own self-interest. We call it economic freedom or market freedom because that is what it offers, the freedom to compete. It is the ability to go out and do those things that will enable you and your family to prosper to the maximum of your ability, but there are some *rules of competition.*

Misinformation has become a normal practice, not only among corporate issuers of securities, but also among financial analysts who support the company's efforts to sell securities, and brokers who mislead uninformed security buyers. I haven't been successful with each of my own investments, but it has been especially irritating when an inexperienced broker (a football coach, no less!) has tried to sell me shares in a company that anyone could see had no significant price appreciation potential. More often than not he was pushing the stock because his company, the brokerage house, had a vested interest in the stock. Well, with three degrees in accounting and finance, I have no excuse for being duped, but I was more than once. I cringe when I hear of the enormous losses families took in the market free fall that started with the dot com companies. It illustrates clearly the plight of millions of investors who put their trust in brokers who turned out to have self-interests greater than their interest in investor's wealth.

Participants in our market economy at the highest level don't seem to under-stand their responsibility for the market that sustains them. Certainly, we can't be accountable for uninformed buyers or sellers when they have had equal opportunity to the knowledge they need. We are responsible when we establish systems so complex that no one other than managers from the inner sanctum of financial institutions can understand. Even if it were not illegal, it would be unethical because they would be affecting choices of people who are not in a position to make an informed judgment. We are back to Warren's "Law beyond the law." We can't really protect the system by more laws alone. That's what Charles Colson said!

The lack of ethical understanding necessary to keep our economy healthy even by our most powerful CEO's is eroding the fundamental structure of the market-place and we must do something about, but what? We must put the system in the hands of people with *moral wisdom* developed over a lifetime of searching for the Law beyond the law. Obviously, this is not a short-term solution, but there is no quick fix. We didn't get in this mess over night or even in one generation. Neither can we slough the matter off on families even though that is where much of one's moral understanding should occur. In addition to family emphasis upon moral training, we need churches to address the issues of human behavior, we need Christian values taught in all schools, and we need Christian leaders throughout society to model moral leadership.

Let me illustrate my concern with a simple example. Suppose I have admired a classic car owned by my neighbor for several years but my neighbor will not sell it. One day he dies, re-kindling my keen interest in the car even greater. After an appropriate time, I go to the widow and tell her I would like to buy the car. She tells me she knows nothing about the car but she will sell it and she asks me to find out how much the car is worth and come back with a value. Wow! What an opportunity for me.

I find out that the car is worth $20,000. I now have to decide what I will offer. If I offer $20,000 and the widow accepts it, I will own a car I have wanted for years and I will have bought it at a true value. The great nebulous economy is not reduced by my offer, the widow's wealth remains as it was but more liquid, and, perhaps most important, I can drive around the city with a clear conscience.

On the other hand, suppose I take advantage of the widow's "uninformed" knowledge of the car and only offer her $5,000. She accepts out of ignorance. Now the great nebulous economy has shrunk by $15,000, the widow's wealth is $15,000 less, and I have gained $15,000 I'm not entitled to according to Adam Smith's rules of competition. Suppose further that I brag to my friends about my great deal, expecting them to congratulate me, but instead they think I am a devious person with whom they will no longer do business. Now I have restricted my ability to compete in the marketplace because I violated Adam Smith's principle of dealing as "an informed buyer with an informed seller."

Many people today will say I am foolish because we are to make the best deals we can as we compete in the marketplace. True, but within the *rules of competition*! It's the rules and our individual responsibility for our economic freedom that corporate executives have forgotten. To coin a phrase: *It's the rules, stupid!* My point is that we are each personally responsible for the market arena in which we compete. It's not rocket science or football. If a football coach does not teach his players the rules, the final score becomes meaningless and the game itself is meaningless. If we do not accept this duty to compete within the rules, we jeopardize the system for everybody.

Multiply my example about the widow by the billions of transactions that take place everyday worldwide. The potential for self-destruction is there. I've already said that more laws are not likely to have much impact on the unscrupulous dealings of market participants. We do need laws, don't misunderstand me, but laws and Adam Smith's principles have little value unless people accept them with the commitment of their *moral sense,* as a commitment to help preserve economic freedom for everyone. The rules need to become part of the soul of every participant. Economic freedom is the structural framework on which we build a market economy, but so is treating everyone fairly within the definition of economic principles.

Was Adam Smith only stating an economic principle or was he re-stating a moral commandment to treat others as we want to be treated? After all, he never claimed to be an economist. He was a preacher and moral philosopher who tied economic activity to its moral base for all time. He was fully aware of the plight of children working in sweatshops in London during the industrial revolution as well as the hard conditions of peasants trying to scratch a living from the leftovers of English nobility. His message to these poor workers, as well as to industrialists and agriculturalist, was that everyone had something to bring to the market, but heed the *rules of competition.* And, true to his calling, he also saw a competitive market as the best say to lift people out of poverty. This allows the economy to grow and maintain balance that is to everyone's benefit. Most importantly, it enables us to live together peaceably in a complex world, unless the crooks among us abort the system.

There is a fundamental teaching in every religion that says, "Love your neighbor as yourself." I'm afraid this has become a trite expression with little meaning to leaders today but it is the absolute bottom line of Christian ethics. It is also the bottom line in our search for the meaning of life and for what constitutes a good life. I am to treat the widow in my previous example, as I would like to be treated. Corporate executives must see that investors get the same information as they want for themselves.

Sometimes Christians take this principle as their own. In truth, it is found in Judaism, Islam, Buddhism, Hinduism, Confucianism, Taoism, and probably every other religion. It actually pre-dates Christianity, even Socrates. It is simply stating what each of us should know through our moral sense. It tells us how to live together and it does not exclude our economic dealings with one another. It is engrained in the structure of our economic relationships because we are all *moral beings dealing as informed buyers and sellers* in every aspect of life, not just economic activities.

In all the publicized illustrations of corporate misconduct, it was usually found that top executives were reaping enormous salaries and other compensation. This is really what triggered public frustration in 2002 and the new laws in the U.S. These powerful economic participants showed no concern for what they were doing to the economy and certainly no concern for the "widow." It was purely and simply self-interest out of control. **GREED!**

We need to instill in business leaders, students, and everybody the need to deal with one another as informed buyers and sellers. It will be a massive change in educational efforts, but we must start if our world is to continue to improve economic opportunities for everyone. Let me point again to the old adage, *"Every society normalizes its own sickness."* If we are to avoid normalizing a decadent way of life, we have to accept our duty as our brother's keeper, even in economic transactions. Understanding this Christian duty can stop the normalization process. All of our freedoms, including economic freedom, depend upon us accepting this important wisdom.

8

LET'S GET REAL, A FEW CASES

Ok, so much for philosophy, editorializing, and reminiscing. Instead, let's walk through a series of cases based on real experiences, not trumped up for illustrative purposes, as a means of dramatizing the issues. Although I will make some comments on each, the cases also give you a chance to make your own judgments about the ethics of the issues. Don't let my thoughts lead you away from your own insight into rightness and wrongness.

A few real experiences (but disguised) may help bring home the ways in which leaders normalize moral sickness—by allowing them to go unchallenged too long or simply by looking the other way. Anecdotes do not prove a hypothesis. I become testy when I see TV newscasters use them to make a larger generalization. In spite of my crabbiness, anecdotes can elevate the reader's awareness of an issue and perhaps lead in the direction of more active leadership in dealing with unethical conduct. Maybe.

◆　　◆　　◆

NATHAN

Nathan, age 22, had graduated from the university in June, 1985 with a 3.5 GPA, which helped him find a prize position with Universe Corp., a progressive manufacturing division of a major corporation, located near the university. He was from a Christian high middle income family, and he had been a positive influence in student government for 4 years. He had an air of assurance that made him a natural leader. He had all the tickets to succeed. Even so, he readily admitted that he was lucky to have found a good job when his classmates were having such a hard time.

In May, 1986, an old and honored employee reported to Travis, Universe General Manager, that Nathan and Kevin, a Universe sales representative, had formed a company through which they were selling business forms to Universe. Kevin's wife was listed as the president of the new company with both Nathan and Kevin listed as officers. Further investigation revealed that Nathan, as a Universe purchasing associate, was sending business form orders to Kevin's wife without getting competitive bids. It was Universe's policy that orders of $1,000 or more must have at least three bidders when they were available. There were plenty of suppliers of business forms available but Nathan evaded the policy by placing several orders less than $1,000 for smaller quantities of the same item.

Universe was forced by the company's Code of Conduct to terminate Nathan and Kevin, but because the company had been charged more than going prices for the forms, headquarters directed the general manager to bring legal charges of fraud against them. Both were convicted and they each received probated prison terms in August, 1986.

Two months after the court decision the whole division was still buzzing. The issue didn't seem to want to go away. In November, 1986, Charles Rudski, Corporate Psychologist, was brought to the division at Travis's request to find out why the issue seemed to be on everyone's mind. Universe had a well-established reputation for taking the high road in managing its business and this was the first experience with such a significant infraction of their Code and certainly with a legal violation. The issue was a constant topic for discussion. People were discussing it at lunch, on breaks, and even on the job. Rudski's assignment was to find out why it was such an intense issue.

Charles' first step was to bring the Purchasing staff together in a meeting to get their feelings and insight before going into other departments. He began the meeting by asking each person to comment on the nature of their relationship with Kevin and Nathan. Everyone seemed quite clear that Kevin had been the instigator and had duped a young naïve new employee.

Jim: Nathan was a likeable fellow. My first contact with him was more social, to get his help to stuff envelopes for our church's pledge campaign. He came by my desk at the close of the day. I picked up a few boxes of paper clips, and we left for the church. Nathan commented that he was glad to see that the company did not mind us using little things like paper clips to help the church. I laughed, realizing how immature young Nathan was, and I told him that the company "helped" a lot of employees with outside projects.

Marie: I took Nathan to lunch to meet my daughter about a month after he came to work. We had a pleasant lunch and didn't get back to the office until about 2:00 o'clock which made him a little uneasy, being so new. I told him that we occasionally took more than an hour for lunch when there were important reasons. I thought he was a sweet, honest, but somewhat impressionable young man, and I was anxious for him to get along with my daughter.

Jerry: I invited Nathan to my Christmas party where we had a conversation about the ABC account. We buy from them all the time, even though their bids are seldom the lowest. Everybody knows that, but we value the quality of their products and their close attention to service. They are fine people and have helped each of us over time with special needs. Nathan was particularly impressed with the CD player they had given Helen and me.

Alvin: When I testified in court, I told them that Nathan had asked me what I thought of the new company he and Kevin were forming to sell to Universe. My comment, which I testified to, was that as long as Universe did not pay more for the forms, it seemed okay. I must admit that I had mixed emotions, but who am I to question someone else's motives? I didn't ask for any details.

Allen: (Purchasing Manager): Alvin, your comment runs through my mind all the time. I see things that I personally feel to be unethical but I don't think I should react to them unless I see clear damage to Universe. I wish Nathan had had enough confidence in me to ask my advice on his venture with Kevin. It was too late when Travis and Martin (owner of a competitive forms supplier) came in and told me the story.

Charles: Well, this has been a good beginning. I think we should go back to our desks now and think about why this episode lingers around so long.

◆　　　◆　　　◆

While Nathan was a student, I considered him a friend, I knew his family, and I wrote a letter of recommendation for him to Travis, General Manager of Universe. I have never been sadder or more deflated over the plight of one of my students than I was about Nathan. The last contact with him was after the lawsuit, just before he left to take a job on an oil rig in the Gulf of Mexico.

Nathan's is a compelling story with which to make a case for the adage, *every society normalizes its own sickness.* Kevin was a 10-year veteran with Universe noted for pushing the rules about as far as one could without breaking them. There was a Code of Conduct in place, which had been passed down from headquarters three years earlier.

I started this book with an opinion that most of the large corporations recently charged with violations of reporting requirements, insider trading, etc. also had ethics statements in place. It is crucial to understand, however, that codes are not a panacea for cures. This is not very insightful on my part but it was the case at Universe. It's an obvious truth that having an ethics document in the desk drawer does nothing. In fact, Travis, the General Manager, tended to be somewhat resentful that it was imposed from headquarters with no input from him or anyone else in his division. I don't blame him, but it was still his job to implement the Code. I suspect that this sort of resentment of ethics from above is not unique to Universe and may contribute to the ethical failures down in the trenches of large organizations. Because it was mostly ignored, the Code was never useful in challenging people at Universe to the high road. Most employees believed their ethical standards were high without reference to the Code. It was a feeling that was fed by Travis' own attitude about the document. It was viewed as an instrument to support the penalty for violations such as Nathan's and Kevin's termination. Actually, there had been no such previous violations as serious as this one.

Earlier I said this normalization process happens over time as leaders take a *passive self-interest* in ethical matters. Let's look at some of those attitudes again:

Everybody does it, so why should I try to stop it?

Note Jim's comments: "I…told him the company 'helped' a lot of employees with outside projects."

Or, Marie's: "…but I assured him it was okay occasionally."

We've always done it. I don't think it does any harm.

Jerry's comment: "Everybody knows that we value their products and services."

I'm not the conscience of the company. It's not my job to blow the whistle.

Alvin: "…as long as Universe did not pay more for the forms, it seemed ok. I must admit that I had mixed emotions but who am I to question someone else's motives? I didn't ask for any details."

Don't break the law, but get the job done.

Allen: "I see things that I personally feel to be unethical but I don't think I should react to them unless I see clear damage to Universe."

I can't tell someone else what is right or wrong for them.

Alvin (again): "I must admit that I had mixed emotions but who am I to question someone else's motives? I didn't ask for any details."

Universe had normalized a moral sickness. They allowed little unethical failures to fester until they grew into a career disaster for Nathan and Kevin. No, I'm not absolving Nathan or Kevin for their indiscretion. They were indeed guilty, but even so, it might have been avoidable, at least for Nathan, if someone had taken the time to talk to him, and the whole company, about the ethics code.

Do you remember my friend the ex-con in my ethics workshop? He's the one who made the cogent point that he would have liked for someone to stop him before he committed a crime that landed him in jail. He was no philosopher but he was right on target. You can call his wish tough love, whistle blowing, or whatever you prefer, but it is an essential part of any sound ethics program. I like to call it loving your neighbor enough to stop him from harming himself. But there is more to be learned here.

When Nathan finished school, I thought he was on his way to a great career with an excellent company. It didn't occur to me that the dearth of ethical training was such a critical issue in our curriculum. Would Nathan have avoided his involvement with Kevin if we had trained him better? I don't know, but I believe deeply that he left school with a hole in his education. Should he have gotten moral training at home? Of course, and he did, but at some point the basic moral values from home and church have to be couched in business situations and I have the unsettling feeling that business schools share this responsibility with businesses themselves.

Was Travis, the general manager, at fault? Absolutely! He should not have filed the Code of Conduct away to get yellow with age. Even though he didn't like having it imposed from above, he was responsible for the ethical conduct of business as stated in the Code, not just his own attitudes about right/wrong. He should have known there was a duty to Nathan and all others to tell them what the rules of competition would be at Universe. And what about the Purchasing Department? They were all good, moral, church-going people. With or without a Code, didn't they have a moral duty to give Universe their best and to practice their faith? Of course, but without leadership even these high sounding traits tend to be put aside.

The reason why employees continued talking about Nathan's and Kevin's termination and conviction is probably obvious to you by this time. There were Code infractions common throughout the company and none of the managers seemed concerned. Why should they be when business was good? Now, with the lawsuit behind them, what should they do about unethical conduct that had been part of their work for years? What was expected from them? From Charles Rudski's report, Travis learned the shocking truth that things "were rotten at Universe." He believed his was a division with high ethical values, which is why he didn't hear about infractions. The truth was that everybody was guilty of a hundred little infractions and no one was telling him. His management style and his business goals just didn't invite people to question others' conduct.

The solution was not easy, but he launched a long term emphasis upon the Code of Conduct that included monthly seminars requiring everyone's participation. He also set up a committee to highlight sections of the Code in the division newsletter and on bulletin boards. But most important, he openly acknowledged his negligence, he said he and the division were going to change. And they did.

In the trial, the judge made a strong point that the prison terms were probated because the company had not given much attention to their own Code and had a degree of culpability. Nevertheless, two careers were damaged severely, probably permanently.

I have looked back at Nathan many times and asked where would he have learned what "conflict of interest" meant? My own search through our curriculum caused a sinking feeling in my stomach.

Ethics in the business law course tended to address what was legal and spent a few sessions on social responsibility as defined by a variety of legislation. The marketing course acknowledged the anti-trust laws, etc. but did nothing to encourage the high road. Accounting courses referred to the professional code of conduct as the standard for public accountants. There was little else in the curriculum that spoke to the matter although several professors said they occasionally had opportunities to point out the ethics of some students' suggestion.

I was struck by one professor's comment that he didn't have time to allow the discussions to go off on tangents. He felt that student's would learn soon enough when they took their first job. Nathan sure did! I have no empirical evidence to support my opinion, but I got a sinking feeling from believing that his was the opinion of too many professors. They, like business executives, see their job as teaching their specialized subject matter, to get the job done. Regrettably, lack of time is all too true in business schools. There never is enough time. But what this means is that we didn't spend enough time and thought on what was really important. What were the priorities? It is part of the issue about the content of business school curricula and the constant pressure for more and more professional training. One might point out that this is too broad a statement to make based on the experience triggered by one student. It isn't just one experience. It comes twenty years later after examining the business curriculum in universities from the broader purpose of using what time we have to prepare students as best we can to:

- contribute to employers in a field of their own interest,

- see business and their careers in the broader sense of how they fit into our social structure, and

- love their neighbors enough to keep them from harm when we can.

In fairness, business schools today do a great deal more to teach ethics but all the programs I know about still teach a secular, consensus ethic. Since the experiences of corporate legal failures in the late 1970's, business schools have honestly tried to inject ethical training into the curriculum. At the time of writing this book, I read an article in the Chicago Tribune about how a number of business schools in large midwestern universities were working on ways to inject ethics into their curriculum. The thirty year old debate still rages. Should there be a separate ethics course, or should ethics topics be included in each course? The distressing thing about the article is that none of the schools seems to address the question of a source for what is ethical. I assure you, none of the schools, other than a few strong religiously based institutions, is looking to God for solutions. Ethics subject matter tends to be either compliance ethics, which says, don't break the law, or do what is "politically correct," which says do what is acceptable to some segment of society. I'm not blaming the business schools because we cannot expect more from schools where education about rightness/wrongness itself is inhibited by law or by social correctness.

In conversation with Nathan's parents, it was apparent that they had done a good job, along with their church, to make Nathan aware of basic moral standards, i.e. "Do unto others what you would have them do to you." But in Nathan's new job, he found other people doing things that caused him twinges of conscience, but he quickly came to believe, with Kevin's help, that he was doing the expected thing. *Nowhere in his education did Nathan have the opportunity to learn about the specific human behavior (or misbehavior) that he would have to face everyday at work and in his social life in a fast-paced world of the upwardly mobile management trainee.*

Where should it have occurred? Who was responsible for Nathan? There are lots of candidates: Kevin, Travis, Allen, the Purchasing Department staff, his parents, his Sunday Schools teacher, his minister, society, and me. Hillary Clinton, in her emphasis on children's development, used to quote an old African saying, "It takes the whole village to raise a child." Nathan and millions of other young people have suffered for the last 30 years because the "village" itself has shunned the understanding of true ethical conduct.

The Book of Proverbs is rich with short, terse bits of wisdom for those who seek to live a good life. Here is an example from Proverbs 14:9-12.

> 9…Fools mock at making amends for sin, but goodwill is found among the upright. 10 Each heart knows its own bitterness, and no one else can share its joy. 11 The house of the wicked will be destroyed, but the tent of the upright will flourish. 12 There is a way that seems right to a man, but in the end it leads to death.

At Universe Corporation, the managers had "mocked" the Code from headquarters and had gradually normalized an unethical environment. This is what eventually trapped Nathan. They would have taken great offense at anyone who suggested that Universe tolerated unethical conduct. Their "house of the wicked" was not destroyed but it came close enough to cause the eventual replacement of the general manager. About eight months after the trial, Travis was transferred. Their way of operating seemed so right, but it surely caused some trauma for Travis, Nathan, Kevin, several department managers, and, to a degree, the whole company.

In the New Testament Letter of James, referred to earlier, there is a subtle bit of wisdom that can make dramatic changes in any organization. It builds upon every person's *moral sense*, which I contend is a part of us from the day we are born. Remember that I referred to one of Thomas Jefferson's letters in which he also said every person has a *moral sense*. But he also said it has to be developed in order to make it useful in directing our lives. James also believed this:

> 21 Therefore lay apart all filthiness and rank growth of wickedness, and receive with meekness the *implanted word*, which is able to save your souls. 22 But be ye doers of the word, and not hearers only, deceiving your own selves. 23 For if any be a hearer of the word, and not a doer, he is like unto a man who observes his natural face in a glass: 24 for he observes himself, and goes his way, and at once forgets what he was like. 25 But he who looks into the perfect law of liberty, and perseveres, being no hearer who forgets, but a doer who acts, he shall be blessed in his doing. (James 1: 21-25)

How does this wisdom from James apply to Universe? They finally came to believe there was unacceptable ethical behavior in their division. The failure to see it earlier had been costly. But they also saw that they had to develop *the implanted word*, the *moral sense*, of those who worked there. When they looked in the mirror, they saw what they wanted to see—a good division in a good company with good people. They didn't ask anyone to a be *doer* of ethical conduct.

As a last word on *Nathan*, think about the words of the Apostle Paul in his letter to the Roman church in which he challenged these new Christians to be cognizant of their *moral sense*.

> When Christians, who are not bound by the Jewish Law, do instinctively what the law requires, they function as the law itself. They show that what the law requires *is written on their hearts (their implanted word)*, and they become witnesses to what the law prescribed. There own conscience bears witness for or against their conduct and they will be judged by God, through Christ, for their inner most secrets of the heart. (Romans 2: 13-16, paraphrased)

Paul was also writing to Travis and all the people at Universe Corp., telling them to build a new understanding among themselves so they would instinctively model the excellent behavior the Code of Conduct (the Law) asked of them.

◆   ◆   ◆

PRENTISS DRESS SHOP

We don't necessarily normalize moral sickness by looking the other way from overt dishonesty. Sometimes just showing kindness to followers can cause bad work habits and become a normal sickness. Consider the case of the *Prentiss Dress Shop*.

Karen Prentiss had owned and operated the Prentiss Dress Shop for 12 years, since she purchased it from the estate of the previous owner in 1979. In the early years, it had provided a good income ranging from $30,000 to $35,000 per year before taxes. She had acquired the business for $90,000. As discount chain and niche stores became more prevalent, particularly the Kaye's Store across the street, profits had declined and were now averaging only about $20,000 before taxes.

Karen operated the store six days a week from 9 am to 9 pm, with six women clerks rotating their schedules between day and night. Helen, the most experienced clerk, had been with the store when it was in the hands of the previous owner. Her husband had been incapacitated for several years and drew $300 a month in disability benefits. Her only son had a small CPA practice in a nearby state.

While Helen knew her job well, increasingly she had been taking off from work for personal reasons. The reasons included such purposes as handling affairs for her husband, visiting her son, preparing for monthly church meetings at her home, getting away from the pressure of the store, and illness. Generally, Karen or one of the other clerks filled in for Helen.

Karen came to believe that she needed to relocate the store to improve her income since many of her customers had moved to the other side of the city. When Glamour Stores offered to buy the business and build a new store in a better location, she was ready to change and accepted their offer of $45,000 without the building. Karen eventually sold the building for $60,000. Karen and all the employees were retained in their positions. After the move, business did indeed pick up and it looked as if Karen had made a good decision. In fact, within 3 months Karen suggested to David Brown, VP for Branch Operations, that they employ an additional clerk. She was not prepared for his response.

"You are right, Karen, we are short-handed but perhaps we should start by replacing Helen. I think she causes an unfair workload for you and the others."

◆   ◆   ◆

Prentiss Dress Shop was caught up in the trend toward chain stores operating niche businesses, particularly in the retail apparel industry. New owners bring new ideas. Really! The demands on employees also change and, even though we like to think family obligations are kept at home out of the workplace, it just isn't so. David Brown is asking Karen to do something about Helen's poor attendance record which should have been handled long ago. Has Helen been doing something that is unethical? Well, she has caused other clerks to work her hours. This can be unethical if they are not really interested in working more hours. If reasons for her absence were taking undue advantage of her long tenure with Prentiss Dress Shop, this would be unethical. If she is asking for favors that other employees don't get, it would be unethical. Everyone, including Helen, tends to miss time at work for valid reasons such as caring for a sick husband, but when these absences are added to an already unacceptable attendance record, it becomes unsatisfactory. Karen has allowed this situation to develop without taking action. She has allowed her *passive self-interest* to normalize a moral sickness.

What should be done now? If Helen were terminated, she would have a good legal case for discrimination against Prentiss Dress Shop because nothing had ever been said to her to indicate dissatisfaction. Besides, it is not the ethical thing to do at this late date. Often students have suggested that Helen be reduced to a part-time schedule, after she has been told why. Most students want the process to start by Karen talking to Helen and explaining why she can no longer be allowed to take off from work as she has been doing. There's a new management with new goals for the store and Karen is not the final authority any more.

The truth is there is no good solution, only the best of bad alternatives. Helen is going to be hurt by anything Karen does. Could it have been avoided? Probably, if Karen had taken a firmer position years ago. Not taking action has led to a bad situation for everyone, and it usually does.

Sometimes troubles away from work can cause good people to lose interest in their jobs, to see it as drudgery, and to find excuses to be somewhere else. Helen is only working out of necessity, not having much fun at work or at home, and not committing her best to Prentiss.

Even so, Karen has also been lax because she has been late with decisions that might have prevented the situation with Helen. Karen is now part of a large organization and she needs to get her act together. I doubt that Glamour Stores will tolerate her *passive self-interest* very long. But the bottom line is her ethical obligation to make sound, timely decisions in the best interest of her new employer and employees. It's also her obligation to the employees in her store. I think God expects it too.

◆   ◆   ◆

BILL WALKER

Most of us remember the scare when Tylenol in several stores was reported to have been laced with poison. We all felt both comfort and admiration when Johnson & Johnson executives made a quick decision to remove Tylenol from shelves all across the country. This episode prompted a different story from a sales executive and a good friend. I will call him Bill Walker.

In 1984, Bill Walker was a sales representative for a pharmaceutical company that had the leading product in its market. The company had a code of ethics and every sales representative, including Bill, knew what it said. It was on the agenda each year at the Annual Sales Meeting and monthly newsletters highlighted various topics from the code. Bill looked at the executives of his company as highly moral people who "walked the talk."

Among the statements in the code was the admonition to sales representatives never to deliberately misrepresent the products or company capability to deliver them to customers. At the August, 1984 Annual Sales Meeting, the company legal counsel told the audience of company executives and sales representatives from all over the world that the leading product had been found to contain a high level of carcinogenic chemicals. He proceeded to tell how his office was going to handle a series of claims that had recently been made by customers under threat of lawsuits.

The President followed the legal counsel with instruction to the sales representatives about how to focus their effort to avoid losing the product market which was about 15% of company sales. He basically said he did not want to misrepresent the product but would not announce details of the claims and would try to settle the claims out of court. He went on to say that company scientists were already looking for ways to remove the harmful agents, but he felt the company had too much to lose to pull the product from the market.

◆   ◆   ◆

If you were Bill Walker, what sense of direction would you get from the meeting? Could you continue to promote sales of the leading product without misrepresenting it? Invariably, students come down on the point that the company was asking its sales representatives to be dishonest, to lie to wholesalers and retailers. Most often, the students want Bill Walker to quit his job. He didn't quit, the company was subject of many law suits, but eventually the product was made safe.

You may want to debate this situation with your friends because it really does challenge us to get business matters into perspective with moral issues. Was there an ethical issue here? Of course there was: the ethical issue was side stepped by the company executives and by sales representatives (including Bill) as they picked up the goal of salvaging the market for the leading product. Of most interest to me was the process that normalized the decision to continue selling a harmful product. The President was saying it was not the task of sales representatives to act as the conscience of their customers. Nonsense! He didn't even want customers to have information with which to exercise their conscience. Doing the right thing can become a secondary issue to executives who can be hurt by a drop in stock prices, etc.

How much profit justifies this kind of deception? In this company, profit on 15% of sales was enough. How much is honesty worth? This may be a hard question for executives who have never faced even the smallest infractions. But if executives operate in a climate in which little indiscretions are not challenged, it is much easier to rationalize the major dilemmas that may come up. Then it becomes easier for the boss to say, *don't break the law, but get the job done.*

This little story reminds me of the John Manville case in the late 1970's when they were indicted in a class action suit for selling asbestos insulation which was also believed to cause cancer. When the smoke cleared, John Manville was a company about 25% of its previous size. But the saddest part of the story came from testimony from company executives who had known for 40 years that asbestos was a cancer causing material. Nevertheless, they continued selling it, became the world's largest supplier of asbestos, and were charged with causing the death or illness of many people. At some point in the past it may have been possible to discontinue the production and sale of asbestos, but not after they had become the world's leader. How many executives do you think might have said: *I'm not the conscience of the company? It's not my job to blow the whistle.*

Yes, leaders are the conscience of the company because they are the one to communicate company policies, traditions, codes and rules, and expectations. If you don't want to be a whistle blower, consider loving those you lead enough to keep them out of trouble.

PROFESSOR HARDMAN

Moral sickness isn't only normalized in businesses. It is rampant in colleges and universities as well. The situation described in this case is real but it has also taken place innumerable times in universities that sponsor intercollegiate athletics.

Harry Hardman, Assistant Professor of American Studies at Major State University, had completed 8 weeks in his first semester on the faculty. He had taught before as a Graduate Assistant, but this was his first tenure track position. He was sitting in his office reflecting upon the mid-term performance of his American Studies 205 class, feeling somewhat self-satisfied. His 24 students had done quite well on the test he had just given with four A's and no one failing. One student, Ron Hasbit, had earned a D but he had put out little effort all term. He had missed 5 of 16 classes, he had not handed in homework assignments, and he had seemed totally bored in class.

As Harry sat thinking about the course, Hasbit knocked on his door. He wanted to talk about the D on the test which he had brought with him. He was quite agitated and blurted out, "I absolutely must have a C. I think I deserve it."

Harry took the test and went over it question by question, showing Ron why his answers were incorrect.

Ron only got more and more agitated and said it was going to be impossible for him to get his grades up by the end of the semester. Harry continued to probe into the matter and asked Ron how he was doing in other classes. It turned out that Ron was failing 3 classes in addition to the D in American Studies 205.

Harry stuck to his guns. He really had no legitimate reason to change Ron's grade. Ron stormed out of the office yelling, "You have not heard the end of this."

Two days later, the coach of the football team dropped by Harry's table in the Faculty Dining Room, ostensibly to meet one of the new faculty members. The conversation soon turned to Ron Hasbit who was the All-State running back having a great year on the football team. The coach told Harry that Ron had not passed enough classes in the past spring to play but he had taken two PE courses in the summer with grades of C in each. The coach said this made Ron eligible, or so he thought. It turned out that the two PE classes were not in Ron's field of study and NCAA had ruled that he had to have a 2.0 average overall to continue to play football. The Athletic Department had to send Ron's fall mid-term grades to the NCAA as a preliminary step to making a final decision immediately after the end of the term.

Harry listened and then said the obvious, "It sounds to me as if Ron's grades in all his classes this fall are too low. I don't think he will make it."

"You are new Dr. Hardman. Talk to Dr. Gregory in Education. He knows we have to make concessions to players if we are going to stay competitive. If we get a bowl bid, it could mean $1 million for the university."

By this time, Harry understood why the coach was in the Faculty Dining Room for the first time all semester. He wanted a favor for Ron, and Harry was getting mad. "Dr. Gregory has nothing to do with my class or the way I grade students, including football players!" With that, Harry left and went to his office and fumed for awhile.

Later in the afternoon, Harry received a phone call from his department chairman. "Harry, you did the right thing with Ron Hasbit. Most of the time, we end up giving these jocks an "Incomplete" grade. You might as well do it too. Don't make a martyr out of yourself."

◆　　　◆　　　◆

How much should a university pay for the objectivity and integrity of its faculty? How much is integrity worth to Harry Hardman?

It is true that universities benefit significantly from bowl appearances, not only in the direct financial payout, but also in recruiting students and even faculty. The pragmatists on every campus quickly point out that compromising on the grades of a few athletes is nothing more than part of the advertising bill. Poor Harry! He was caught in the middle of one of the great debates on campuses of NCAA member schools, not to mention among sports enthusiasts. Does the need to compete in intercollegiate sports compromise the purpose of universities? It did at Major State. And it does in many universities. Even if we are magnanimous enough to call it sports "advertising," what it advertises (communicates) does not always contribute to the institutional educational purposes. In many cases the antics of athletes give the opposite impression that education, studying, learning, and integrity are of minor importance.

Then, there is Harry Hardman. What does the university owe him? When he tries to teach students within the purposes of the institution, doesn't the institution have an obligation to support him? When the department chairman says, "Don't make a martyr out of yourself," isn't he saying, don't let ethics and integrity get in the way of such things as Harry's tenure and promotions?

What about Ron Hasbit? Even if he completes his education, what is he taking with him? An attitude that the world owes him whatever he needs? Will he learn what it takes to create a worthwhile life? I don't think so.

◆　　　◆　　　◆

Richard Niebuhr, in his book *The Responsible Self,* considers the manner in which the word *responsible* has replaced other words we once used, such as *moral* and *good.* We now talk about responsible citizens, responsible students, or responsibilities of the office. More often than not, we once would have said moral citizens, good students, or the moral obligations of the office. In the last sentence of the section entitled, "The Meaning of Responsibility," Niebuhr says, "…I shall simply ask that we consider our life of response to action with the question in mind, 'To whom or what am I responsible and in what community of interaction am I myself?'" If we conclude that we are responsible to God, we are getting close to *moral wisdom.*

He is arguing for a concept of Christian ethics in which we are asked to pursue the teachings of Christ and acknowledge our responsibility to God. This is the essence of Christian ethics, a revealed ethics. Is there any higher calling? Doesn't this put demands of the workplace in a clearer perspective of subservience to our offer of eternity?

9

THE CHURCH, IT'S STILL A PLAYER

Some months ago, a newspaper editorial claimed that the *myths* of the Bible have outlived their usefulness in dealing with today's immorality. Well, there are some Biblical stories that challenge logic, but the Bible is not about logic, it is about our evolving faith over 4,000 years. It has to be read from the perspective of the understanding of the people who lived the stories at the time. The newspaper editor used his concept of Biblical mythology to make the points that immoral conduct is a social matter and no greater today than it was during the Middle Ages. Of course, he was talking about the Crusades, the Inquisition, the indulgences of the church, racial discrimination, and the heavy-handed treatment of the poor throughout history. He compared these injustices to the many government programs today aiding the poor, to the United Nations and other organizations working to avoid war, and to safety and environmental ordinances, etc. Rising incidents of unethical conduct in business and government, to the editor, were only products of better media coverage.

It was a thought-provoking editorial, but missed the point that we are supposed to grow in our understanding of right and wrong, not just maintain middle-age standards of conduct. Nor did he address issues of divorce and lack of marriage commitment, waste of natural resources, and abuse of power by executives and elected officials.

The editor was right on one point, that our racial attitudes are better today. Nevertheless, most people involved in racial issues today tell us we are at the point where we need to change attitudes, not just the public institutions that serve us. This sounds a lot like a need to get more commitment to the commandment to love our neighbor as ourselves. In other words, it means our moral sense needs upgrading. We not only need to elevate our attitudes about race, but about all aspects of human behavior. We also need to develop our moral sense continually and take it with us into our highly systemized and organized professional lives. The church needs to be in the mix!

Why shouldn't we expect conduct to be *better* today, not just as good as the Middle Ages? With all the wisdom we have accumulated throughout history, shouldn't we expect our moral wisdom to be on a higher level today? Aren't we expected to grow in our faith, in our search for God's will, and in our own will to "love one another"? Sorry, Mr. Editor, but the Bible is far more than a book of mythology.

The editor is only one of many voices today expressing disappointment with Christians' narrow-minded concept of morality. We are charged with wanting to make our own Christian ethic the standards for the world. Right on! It's not that we don't recognize goodness in the expectations of other faiths. Rather, it should be our belief that goodness in individuals isn't achieved without the inner voice coming from God. If goodness is a matter between each person and God, a constant search for God's will in each of our personal lives, then it's not enough to rely entirely on laws, codes, rules, or +political correctness. We have to take responsibility ourselves.

Other prominent people in positions to sway public attitudes share the editor's idea that we can develop a workable consensus morality, e.g. many college professors, social advocates, political junkies, TV and radio talk show hosts, commentators, and a large number of people grown up in the "baby boom" and "generation x."

A growing number of opinion shapers today espouse the attitude that we can do it ourselves; we don't need a mystical God to tell us what is right or wrong. Too often, these opinions come from people like the editor, who see all the social institutions that do good work, but fail to look inward at the individual whose moral sense says anything goes. Truthfully, we also hear this theme from people who talk about the need for faith, the church, mosque, or synagogue, and a return to traditional family values. We have indeed established a wide range of organizations, private and public, to respond to human needs and to unethical and immoral conduct. The editor was right from this viewpoint.

What about changing the attitudes we hold in our private lives when we are not restrained by law or political correctness. How do we get leaders (everyone, really) who make life-changing decisions to look for the high road in their professional lives? Can we really improve conduct by adding more laws to the books or forming more social agencies and organizations? Wouldn't it be better to change lives early, especially lives of future leaders, before they get into the *passive self-interest syndrome?* I think so, and this is where the church can play its role most effectively. No, I don't see the church taking on the bureaucracy of government, business, or any large organization, but it is still possible to affect the lives of those who lead these monstrous organizations today, but especially the moral sense of those coming through the pipeline. If we gained nothing else from proper religious education, we could surely save enormous amounts of money and other resources. But there is more to be gained.

I believe it is important for Christians in the 21st century to take a hard look at the role of their church, both the universal church and each local congregation, in preparing future leaders to deal with immorality on a daily basis. Philosophical concepts of morality and ethics are not enough; they must be absorbed into our souls. We only need to look at the history of civilizations and nations who allowed their value structure to deteriorate to see the sense in our Christian ethic.

There was Socrates, for instance, who through his endless questions, concluded that morality was a hopeless search without some higher authority. His questions were intended to push his listeners to acknowledge the need for a higher authority. He was a polytheist who concluded that, without a higher authority, a society based upon personal morality could not succeed. It took 700 more years before God came, walked among us, and showed us the higher authority.

Was God using Socrates, among so many others, who were searching for goodness? If God had preceded Paul to Greece, it seems logical that He can also precede efforts to develop a higher sense of morality in our systematized world. Without such an authority, there will always be an abundance of scoundrels plying their own notion of right/wrong. Indeed, we do need a higher authority to provide the moral goal in our treatment of others. This opens the place for the church today that has been much too timid in helping us define rightness and wrongness.

I say this with a sense that there is already a moral awakening today. You see it in the increase in religious movies, in discussions of religion on talk shows, in debates on the relationship of government to religion, and in renewed interest in the Bible. The problem is that it comes from outside the church causing church leaders to be reactive rather than proactive. This is a deep concern. Without the direction from the church, as Jesus foresaw it, the new religious fervor can lead to misunderstanding about God's purpose and even more splintering.

Well, forget about the editor for a moment. The most disturbing voice about the impotence of the church is now coming from concerned Christian ministers themselves. Many Christians, theologians and laypersons alike, accuse the church, especially the "high church," of failing to preach and teach the Gospel of

Christ. As I listen to my pastor speak out, I am convinced that his concern is at the heart of the church's failure to speak out on the moral issues that face us. His view is that too many local churches no longer teach Christ as the Son of God and consequently they have watered down their position and have adopted "political correctness" in their ministry. True! True! You see this is at the heart of what we call the Christian ethic. Rightness or wrongness to Christians is learned from the teachings and the example of Christ, not from laws or social correctness. If we are to live by His example, it seems imperative that we know Him to be "God walking among us." This makes His word authoritative and believable.

THE CHURCH IS LATE, BUT THE PARTY IS STILL GOING

My own beef with the church is not because I have reduced the faith to mythology, as did the editor. Rather, it is what happens to Christians after they take the "faith leap" and acknowledge Christ as the Son of God. It has always seemed to me that there is a break in our understanding of the connectors between Jesus' two great commandments, i.e. *love God and love your neighbor as yourself.* We are engrained with the first commandment, love God, but as we get older and move into the systemized professional world, the second commandment gets lost. Then, young people see this lack of respect for Jesus' second commandment and conclude it is less important. I think it is caused by too little effort to grow Christians. I'm talking about education, Christian education!

It is like our brain where we have cells that receive information, cells that store information, others that take information and use it for a variety of decisions, and connectors between all of them. However, if the connectors between brain cells are damaged or not in place, the information received is of little value. When we receive and accept the information that we are to *love God*, it should motivate Christians to do something with it, i.e. to *love our neighbors.* But the connectors are not strong enough, and too many Christians are not making the connection. They need help from the one who "brung them to the dance,"—the church.

Elton Trueblood, in his Book, *The Future of the Christian,* 1971, addressed this disconnect directly. The theme of his book was,

> *Christians cannot survive in the future without gathered fellowships (churches), but we need to examine more rigorously the central purpose of repeated gatherings.*

We are called together, not primarily to attend a meeting of worship, but, far more, to share in a meeting for the preparation for the ministry of common life.

In other words, churches bring people together to worship, sure, but mostly to develop the connectors between worshiping God and ministering to our neighbors. Today, this latter duty has been relegated to social agencies and government, and for all the good they do, these agencies cannot make people good. Consequently, we keep experiencing aberrations in the Christian ethic to love our neighbors. When we leave our Christian duty in the hands of social organizations, we seem to take a self-satisfied look in the mirror and say I've done enough. We leave it to the social *system*! There's that word again. The result is a life dominated by self-interest. It is a small next step to begin exercising self-interest in unethical and illegal ways.

As pointed out earlier, Christian ethics means the kind of life exemplified by Christ, taught by him, and reported to us in the New Testament. If so, we need to know what He exemplified and taught in order to offer our Christian ethics to the world where decaying ethical standards is evident all around us. Well, I'm not a theologian (which is obvious), merely an educator and a concerned people-watcher. I'm not a major league baseball player either, but I know when the batter strikes out. *I think the church has struck out in its commission to take the faith to others and teach them how to live the Christian ethic.*

Thankfully, growing numbers of people are more concerned today than ever about the decadent direction of society. This is a hopeful sign and creates an opportunity for the church to get back into the game. At least, we are seeing a moral awakening in society, a moral awareness, if not yet a moral backbone.

Many ethicists also tell us that we are becoming more moral, at least in our awareness of evil and mistreatment of other humans, just as the editor said. What they mean is we are conforming to social standards of conduct at a higher level today. It would be a good thing, except that most empirical studies of social behavior tell us our conduct today is measured by socially agreed-upon standards, not by moral philosophy and certainly not yet by Christian ethics. Thus, none of these consensus standards come close to universal acceptance. It is a consensus ethic that changes from one subset of society to another over time, and with shifting self-interests. This opens the door to business executives and government officials, who harbor the passive self-interest attitude that, "We have always cut corners or looked away from bad conduct," or "Everybody does it so why bother correcting it now," or "It's not my job to make employees moral, just to get the work done."

It is sad that the church, our moral agent, has been relegated to the sidelines watching the erosion of our moral fiber. It is no longer viewed as arbiter of right and wrong, as it once was. If the Supreme Court continues to have its way, we are not going to regain our moral heritage.

Certainly the disconnect between the church and the world of leaders is worth our attention. Information fed into our souls and brains on Sunday morning ought to have some relevance to the workweek. I don't want to make broad charges that are not universally correct or accepted. Many churchmen do speak out to address a whole list of bad conduct in our society. So what am I talking about? For one thing, the voices only tend to show up after the fact, reacting to some tragic event. Even then, there is no unified voice. Christians have a right to expect the church to lead us away from immoral lifestyles before the fact. Ministers do indeed address moral decadence in their sermons, innumerable religious books speak to the issue, and there does seem to have been a renewed interest in religion in the 1990's. So, where's the beef? What more do we want from the church? Think about these expressions that we often hear:

1. "People of all religions worship the same God. They have to make their own moral decisions."

2. "I don't see what Jesus contributes to the mix. We just need to be good."

3. "I enjoy going to Sunday School. I like to see my friends and find out what's happened during the week."

4. "I grew up believing a lot of things were sinful. I'm glad we've gotten away from those old-fashioned ideas."

5. "If I don't hang out with my friends and do as they do, they aren't going to have anything to do with me. Having friends is the most important thing."

6. "If I'm going to keep my job, I have to do as I'm told whether I agree or not."

From these attitudes, we read that the church, even as Christ's body of believers, has gradually shifted toward a social ministry (a social gospel) of consensus expectations. People in the fundamentalist persuasions charge that many of the "high churches" have become tradition bound and don't teach the Word of God. Then, there is the opposite view that fundamentalist local churches have become bound to the literal Bible but are weak in applying their faith to the needs of the world around them. Each of these attitudes reflects what Elton Trueblood called "pietists" and "activitists" in another of his books, *The New Man for Our Time,* 1970. He used the terms to refer to people who could bring different interests and competences to the church, all of which are needed. However, these attitudes also tend to polarize the universal church with many denominations holding up their brand of religion as the *right* religion.

As we describe the activities of church members, I suspect that individual members of any church expect more church effort in the area of their personal interest. They don't get to the issue of why the church has become a less potent force in the world because they have formed their own opinions about what the world needs and they don't want their church to get involved. But, most of all, I sense that not even active church members are anxious to see their church meddling in matters of business, government, education, etc., except to get money from these institutions. Even so, behind all these types of comments, there seem to be three generalizations about why the church is searching for its proper role in our workaday lives.

I—THE DIVIDED CHURCH AND NORMALIZED MORAL SICKNESS

There is no denying the *church divided* that we hear about so much today. We are split in doctrine, in worship practices, in ministerial training, in mission emphasis, and even in recognition of God, who "walked among us." Baptists debate literal verses broad interpretations of the Bible, Catholics have been damaged by abusive priests and their rigid interpretations of the place for women in pulpits, Episcopalians and Methodists are struggling with homosexuality among their priests, and similar issues beset most of the major denominations. None of us can afford "holier than thou" thoughts. If you watch the news long enough, it becomes apparent that all denominations have troubles in their midst.

In truth, the divided church has been the reality of the Christian faith at least since the Roman Catholic and the Eastern Orthodox churches excommunicated each other in the 4th century. In a broad sense, the large and growing number of denominations and independent churches are merely Christians exercising their freedom to determine their own truth. Yet, Jesus only referred to "my church," not churches. Paul at first seemed to believe he was changing Judaism, not forming a different faith. Jesus, Paul, and other apostles admonished the early church to resist "false prophets" or "false teachers." The "false prophets" for the most part were believers in Judaism or other religions or philosophies who had a different idea about how the doctrine of the new faith was to fit into long-standing traditional faiths. Perhaps some were opportunistic, but many were also well-intended prophets and teachers of Judaism. So even from the beginning, there were different interpretations of doctrine and, over the centuries, other good people who think differently, who have a different view of Christ's church, have chosen to go their own way. Has it been a bad thing or a good thing?

Perhaps, though, the movement away from traditional denomination affiliation to independent local churches is the most serious division among Christians. It has gained momentum because it is the child of devout Christians, not rabble-rousers, who feel that "high church" denominations have lost sight of the purpose of the church.

To the extent that the constant mutating effect creates more churches and attracts more Christians, we can argue that it is a good thing. We have to admit that the past missionary zeal of churches of all denominations did indeed create growth. But, in order to gain new members, did we water down the example and teachings of Christ? In the competition among denominations, as it progressed into the 20th century, did we "de-claw the tiger?" Did we minimize the call to Christians to develop *moral wisdom*? Did we soft-peddle the expectations of Christianity in order to alleviate personal conflict for members in the workplace? I think so.

What does this have to do with Christian ethics and the normalization of moral sickness? A great deal. If leaders of the church or its many denominations can't agree on how to present the Bible to those who need it, what chance do mere mortals have? Is political "spin" any different from lying? Is lying a sin for students and merely a social indiscretion for government officials or business executives? Is it merely trade practice for used car salespersons to fluff out their cars and not for stockbrokers to do the same for the securities they sell? Is premarital sex a sin for prostitutes on the street but not for executives, legislators, highly paid athletes, and entertainers away from home? Is homosexuality a sin for everyone other than ministers? How are churchmen going to make these judgments without coming to grips with the reliability of the Bible? In other words, what authority do we use to resolve immoral conduct if not the teachings of the One who is the corner stone of our faith, who provided the fundamental teachings, and who exemplified a "worthwhile life?" As a long-time teacher, it seems to me we are talking about learning, education, *growing in our faith*.

If we accept the notion that Christianity is grounded on the idea of developing the *moral wisdom* of believers, it obviously has to be taught or absorbed in some way. Perhaps it is better to point out that wisdom, moral or otherwise, will be absorbed, for better or worse. It is simply the task of the church to make sure that what is absorbed is truly *moral wisdom*, as Christ taught.

I have to be honest. From what I see, the united church's frayed edges are coming apart. I am a Methodist because I am still a bit tradition bound and I feel I have to be something, but I wish it were not so. However, being an ecumenical person doesn't mean you simply ignore the development of moral wisdom, but how do we span the many doctrines on moral wisdom? Well, as naïve as it may sound, our Christian ethic places the duty on each of us to search the scriptures of the New Testament for answers rather than put them to a vote or agree among our friends. I never said I didn't have a few foibles (a few?).

Most every Christian understands the problem. If, by some magical process, we could bring denominations together, we each would want it to look like our own idea of a good church. I would want all other denominations to become Methodists. There is need and room for some level of doctrinal difference but there is a missing foundation on which we must agree. The mode of transportation by the Israelites crossing the Red Sea may not be critical, but the fact of their making the pilgrimage as a mass of humanity led by God is important. Jesus' birth to a virgin is subject to question, but the arrival of the Christ is imperative. We can rationalize each miracle in the Bible but, if we study it in totality, we can't deny the hand of God in the lives of all those characters (leaders) of the Bible. Nor should we forget that the story of Christ's people did not end in the Book of the Revelation. It was intended that the church continue to move forcefully in the world to baptize, make disciples, and provide *instruction*. The truth that makes us free comes from *moral wisdom* and, unless I have wasted my academic career, wisdom still comes from study, education, instruction, and experience.

As said earlier, the normalization of moral sickness happens when leaders ignore or rationalize the little indiscretions that happen each day. It also happens when church leaders, professional and otherwise, allow secular practices to permeate the teachings of the church. "Everybody else does it," so why shouldn't the church.

II—BIG BUSINESS IS TOO BIG FOR THE CHURCH

When we compare the localized thrust of churches with the enormous growth and complexity of corporate America and the massiveness of government, it is easy to understand why the influence of local churches is so easily sloughed off. It would be unfair to expect church leaders to understand the complexities that often befuddle business executives themselves. But, conversely, leaders of industry can benefit from intensive study of the Christian ethic. It is important to understand the manner in which corporate planning and management tends to absorb the minds of managers deep inside corporate organizations *to the exclusion of moral considerations.* The weight of decisions necessary to carry out business plans is far greater than the anemic challenges of their church, even for executives or administrators who do attend church regularly. Professional managers do not easily interpret the Sunday morning message into challenges for their organizations, the rules of competition are out of bounds for church consideration, and let's just let sleeping dogs lie. But church leaders can help overcome these problems.

This part of the problem for the church has been the subject of much of this book but especially Chapter V and VI. Large corporations have developed a mystique about themselves that baffles even the brightest investigators, lawyers, and financial analysts. As I have said, there is no reason to assume that anyone outside the world of corporations will fully understand them.

But let's not forget that corporations are big because they have met a need. Perhaps, it would be more accurate to say they provide what we want, whether we need it or not. They have enabled us to utilize our natural and human resources most effectively to meet demand for products and services until now when we are squandering natural resources causing vicious debate among social antagonists. The appropriate cliché here is, *Let's not throw the baby out with the bath water.*

However, as awesome as many corporations may seem, they are still staffed by mere humans; people who are less than perfect and who need guidance, no matter what their level of authority in the firm. Like all successful ventures, corporations can be and have been abused by imperfect people. The abuse has been by individuals, mortal human beings, who are not too big to benefit from church teachings. I said in the beginning that I'll bet the executives of Enron, World-com, ImClone, Arthur Anderson, and most other troublemakers were active to some degree in a church. My guess is that each of them also came from good families who had some contact with a church. I also said they didn't commit their mischief for the first time when they got caught. Where was the church when these corporate scoundrels were growing up and when they were progressing through corporate organizations? It was much too late to provide moral training after they were indicted or charged with crimes. Moral wisdom was needed all along the way to keep them out of jail and keep corporate America's image above doubt, and that's the church's job.

The church may not be able to tackle large complex organizations directly, but it can encourage individual executives to follow the high road. Equally possible is that the church can begin to improve its educational arm to strengthen the moral sense of beginning leaders before they face the challenges of systemized America. Human behavior can be changed. It isn't necessary for church leaders to understand "Discounted Cash Flow." They only need to lift up the teachings of Christ regularly for people who do measure investments with discounted cash flow measurements. Middle managers who worry about their status with the boss also need to be concerned about their status with God. Families of middle managers need to understand how dad (or mom) gets the money to support them. Each member needs be involved in the tough decisions to the extent they are old enough or capable of participating. It will be a lot easier to face up to conduct middle managers feel to be unethical or illegal, if the family already knows the situation and is willing to accept the consequences. Families, supported by a potent church, can only strengthen leaders who deep down know right from wrong.

III—MORAL WISDOM HAS TO BE TAUGHT

Anyone who attends church, even infrequently, has heard many times that Christianity is founded upon the belief that Jesus was the Son of God. Yes, but so what? Where is the connection between this fundamental belief and our charge to live morally and ethically? Does it have any affect on decisions in corporate offices or in the halls of government? Without seeing a connection, all too often, after this affirmation of faith, well-meaning Christian executives meekly accept the idea that morality in our faith is a nice Sunday morning subject and is the same as other major faiths. If you ask most people what is meant by Christian ethics, they usually answer that it is not different from any other ethics. Well, if this is true, why do we need to defend Jesus as the Son of God? Why not join with the Jews and Muslims, return to religious legalism, and pray to the One God? Or why not accept Socrates' search for a worthwhile life and quit bothering with any form of worship of one god. Not enough Christians think about the impact of "God walking among us" on the ethical values that guide us.

My big point has been that we usually let normalization of moral sickness happen because we assume certain conduct to be ethical or moral without reference to any authority higher than ourselves. Leaders allow bad conduct because they are not firmly anchored to any moral standard other than consensus driven standards. Even so, let me be fair. There are "societies" including business organizations, educational institutions, churches, governmental agencies, and our circles of friends in which leaders do defer to God's will. Some years ago, a friend who was the human resource director for a local government, made no bones about his emphasis upon candidates' religious conviction. We sometimes hear of government officials holding voluntary prayer meetings. We hear of some companies holding prayer services. Private colleges and universities, and occasionally public institutions, hold religious services and even offer institutional worship. On public campuses, it is usually organized by students but is frequently attended by faculty. Then there are a growing number of Bible study groups outside church auspices. So, it can be done.

However, there is always lurking in the background the question of what is legally possible today in our religious practices. Then, all these religious activities tend to be tangential to the main purpose of the organization. There is no clear connection. Spiritual programs seem to be viewed as a fringe benefit unrelated to work. The preponderance of organizations still tends to follow consensus opinion as the ultimate determinant of right from wrong. What else should one expect in our secular legalistic society?

Even a cursory reading of the Old Testament makes clear the historic tie between the faith of Israel, based on the Mosaic Law, and the nation of Israel. The descendents of Abraham first became God's chosen people by their faith in Jehovah and later they became the nation of Israel. This rich heritage is still very much evident in Israel today where there are close ties between the politics of Israel and their faith, Judaism.

We refer to countries in the Middle East, Africa, and Southeast Asia as Islamic countries because their people are closely guided by Islamic Law emanating from the Koran. Islam, the religion, provides the ethical and social standards in their part of the world. Religious sects such as the Shiites and the Sunnis are also political parties. While both Jews and Muslims believe firmly in their individual privilege to determine right from wrong, individual interpretations have evolved from a long history with their law, traditions, and priestly teachings. In other words, their religious ethic has flowed from a rich heritage of law into today's practices of the people.

Christianity has a different history. Thanks mostly to the work of Paul, Christianity lost its nationalistic ties early in it history. From the *Epistle of Mathetes*, AD 130,

> For the Christians are distinguished from other men neither by country, nor language, nor the customs, which they observe. For they neither inhabit cities of their own, nor employ a peculiar form of speech, nor lead a life that is marked out by any singularity...

Paul made it the faith of all people, as Jesus intended. It is not dependent upon support of any country.

The United States was the first nation to organize its government explicitly to separate religion from government. However, it was not so much to eliminate the influence of the church on leaders of government, as it was to keep government out of church affairs. Why did our founding fathers take the bold step? They did it to make sure that the new country allowed people the freedom to pursue their religion just as the New Testament promises. In addition, they were also committed to the idea that the United States was to be a "Christian nation." It was not a well-defined concept, but, as a minimum, the original intent of the Founding Fathers was that we would be a people dedicated to a Christian ethic. As I pointed out, Jefferson always maintained that mankind was endowed with a *moral sense*. In a letter to Peter Carr in 1787, he said,

> "He who made us would have been a pitiful bungler, if he had made the rules of our moral conduct a matter of science. For one man of science, there are thousands who are not. What would have become of them? Man was destined for society. His morality, therefore, was to be formed to this object...The *moral sense*, or conscience, is as much a part of man as his leg or arm. It is given to all human beings in a stronger or weaker degree, as force of members is given them in a greater or less degree. It may be strengthened by exercise, as may any particular limb of the body."

This was a lifelong belief for Jefferson who had so much to do with the shaping of our "three-headed government." The Apostle Paul had a similar thought about man's special relationship to God in creation.

1 Corinthians 15:16-19

> For if the dead do not rise, then Christ is not risen. And if Christ is not risen, your faith is futile; you are still in your sins! Then also those who have fallen asleep in Christ have perished. If in this life only we have hope in Christ, we (*Christians*) are of all men the most pitiable. NKJV (italics by the author)

Jefferson, observing the need for a moral sense to enable men and women to live together, and Paul, observing the need for Christians to accept the resurrection, came to the same conclusion. Mankind holds a special place in God's plan for his creation. Later, in 1816, in one of the continuing exchanges of letters with John Adams, Jefferson had this to say,

> I believe...that (justice) is instinct and innate, that the *moral sense* is as much a part of our (being) as that of feeling, seeing, or hearing; as a wise Creator must have seen to be necessary in an animal destined to live in society.

Well, you might suspect a graduate of Mr. Jefferson's University will give great credence to his wisdom. I have to admit I didn't always recognize Mr. Jefferson's significance at the University of Virginia. In my first year there, on Founders Day, the announcement was made that classes would be suspended until noon, probably to encourage attendance at a ceremony on the grounds. I had not heard of Founders Day at other schools getting such attention so I asked a professor why it was so important. His astonished look told me I was in deep trouble. He pointed out, as I slipped under the table, that "The University" was founded by Mr. Jefferson. He suggested that I spend several hours researching the subject and writing 1,000 words about Mr. Jefferson's University. From that day, I have had a keen interest in what Mr. Jefferson said.

But his wisdom also had enormous weight with the founding fathers, not just me. His belief in the existence of each person's *moral sense* led him to press for a government with power entrenched ultimately in the governed. His wisdom has been in the background of our country's heritage from the beginning. And most importantly, it is not inconsistent with the teaching of the New Testament.

This is getting to the point. Too many people seem to be looking for a law, code, or some kind of directive that says one thing is wrong and something else is right. As we have lost confidence in leaders, we have attempted to create laws, codes, rules, and conventions to replace leadership in our daily lives. We no longer trust leaders' judgment. Many people in the financial community think insider trading laws are vague and they look for the minimum standards to dictate their decisions. The law limiting stockholder's responsibility for the debts of their corporations had to be strengthened because executives were interpreting it narrowly and acting irresponsibility. Young people today are quick to point out that extramarital sex is not illegal, therefore it is acceptable behavior. Employees take advantage of sick leave policies whether they are sick or not because it is not illegal. We feel more secure relying on the law, codes, or rules rather than on the *moral wisdom* of our leaders.

We do need a legal system to maintain a degree of order, but it will not make us moral. I might add that until we do make more people moral, the order in society will always be in jeopardy. Too few people, even leaders, seem to have much confidence in the *moral wisdom* of the individual that Jefferson believed in so ardently. Perhaps John Adams was right. Maybe we do need strong central government, police, elaborate sets of laws, and people to determine right conduct for us. Sorry, I don't believe it, Mr. Adams, and I wouldn't believe it if I had attended Harvard.

Let me say it again. Christianity has always been a faith based upon *moral wisdom*. Consistent with Jefferson's opinion, we expect religion to be the source for development of the *moral sense*. Our national Constitution and the organization of our government intentionally leave room for interpretation so we can truly be a government by the governed in search of *moral wisdom*. This is where power in the United States is supposed to be vested—in the governed. Now consider, for instance, the Parable of the Mustard Seed, Matthew 13: 31-32:

> He told them another parable: "The kingdom of heaven is like a mustard seed, which a man took and planted in his field. Though it is the smallest of all your seeds, yet when it grows, it is the largest of garden plants and becomes a tree, so that the birds of the air come and perch in its branches."

It is not a stretch to interpret the mustard seed to be Jefferson's *moral sense*. The parable tells us it is to grow just as Jefferson said, "...it may be strengthened with exercise..." If so, isn't it logical that the place to develop moral wisdom starts at home in families supported by the church with strong educational programs teaching Christian ethics?

Law, traditions, codes, and customs do not bind Christians. The police, the courts, and other authorities do this to maintain order. Christians are bound to higher standards by their own *moral wisdom*, which leads them to understand and believe the commandment to love one's fellowman. Please interpret this correctly. *It doesn't mean Christians can ignore the law at any level.* Quite the contrary, we are commanded to obey the laws that give us order and direction, but equally important is our duty to contribute to productive laws that enable us to live in society. And, yes, we must also work within the systems of society to change laws that we do not believe to be just.

For Christians, ethical standards must be proactive, meaning the law of the land is expected to come out of the ethical standards of the people. Through the exercise of our individual *moral wisdom*, we come together and reach consensus on laws that benefit society, not the other way around.

This is a dangerous concept when we remember that even crooks have a vote. Nevertheless, individuals exercising their moral wisdom are not promoting sedition or even non-violent protest, although it does not exclude protest. It is promoting God's guidance in our relationships with our fellowman. Christians are motivated by the example and teachings of Christ, not by laws. It is worth repeating. This type of faith leads to *moral wisdom*. We don't wait for the law, not even moral law, if it is posed to us as coming from consensus judgment.

In this context, we need to examine Jesus' teachings such as found in Matthew 5:17-20:

> "Do not think that I have come to abolish the Law or the Prophets; I have not come to abolish them but to fulfill them. I tell you the truth, until heaven and earth disappear, not the smallest letter, not the least stroke of a pen; will by any means disappear from the Law until everything is accomplished. Anyone who breaks one of the least of these commandments and teaches others to do the same will be called least in the kingdom of heaven, but whoever practices and teaches these commands will be called great in the kingdom of heaven. For I tell you that unless your righteousness *surpasses* that of the Pharisees and the teachers of the law, you will certainly not enter the kingdom of heaven.

Jesus made this statement to a Jewish audience who wanted him to be the earthly, political king who would throw off the shackles of Rome and make Judea a free entity among world nations, even a world power. If we read only the phrase, "I have not come to abolish (the Law or the Prophets), but to fulfill them," it does indeed sound like the start of insurrection. This was not to be the case. Read also, "For I tell you that unless your righteousness *surpasses* that of the Pharisees and the teacher of the law, you will certainly not enter the kingdom of heaven." The key word is "*surpasses*." This puts our accountability squarely on shoulders of everyone hoping for the kingdom of God, not on the laws of governments or even the laws of God's people.

It is an awesome responsibility. We are accountable to God for developing our moral sense into a moral wisdom. Wow! It's scary until we read further into Jesus' words while he was on earth. In John 14: 15-21 Jesus promised help from a Counselor who will be with us forever.

> "If you love me, you will obey what I *command.* And I will ask the Father, and he will give you another Counselor to be with you forever—the Spirit of truth. The world cannot accept him, because it neither sees him nor knows him. But you know him, for he lives with you and *will be in you.*"

Who is this Counselor? Jesus said he *"will be in you,"* a Counselor within us speaking through a moral sense, our soul. What more do we need to know? In this report of Jesus' words, we also see that he asks us to keep his commandments. However, the only commandments he gave us were broad and even nebulous, i.e. to love God and to love our neighbor. In Matthew 22:37-40:

> Jesus replied: Love the Lord your God with all your heart and with all your soul and with all your mind.' This is the first and greatest commandment. And the second is like it: 'Love your neighbor as yourself.' All the Law and the Prophets hang on these two commandments.

Within these broad duties, we are left with a great responsibility to exercise *moral wisdom* in all of life and *it does not exclude the workplace.*

Let's put it all together. Our commandment to love everyone, even our enemies, is given to us with the assurance that we can call on a Counselor within at any time for guidance in knowing what to do. We were not given rules, codes, conventions, or specific laws. Rather we have the *moral wisdom* to imitate Christ in all our transactions, business and otherwise. *What would Jesus do?* We have the means to know, even in the complex corporate offices of powerful decision-makers.

Jesus also said we would have the Counselor with us *forever* meaning throughout our lives, even in the office. Our moral sense is the connector between the Counselor and our workaday brain. Some people look at life as a time of testing to determine our qualifications for the kingdom of heaven or perhaps an opportunity to earn entry. Well, we can't earn what is already given, but the idea of life as an opportunity comes close, if we look at life as an opportunity to show love for God and love of our fellowman. If you prefer to view life as a test period in one's existence, so be it, as long as we are not trying to earn God's approval. We build our lives upon this foundation—a life of *moral wisdom* learned from a life of testing and searching. It sounds like the school of hard knocks, doesn't it? It is! It shapes how we view our self-interest in business transactions or how we relate to government-generated resources. It strengthens leaders to overcome their passive self-interest and respond to the little indiscretions that occur around them. We build trust with others as they learn to accept our *moral wisdom*. In addition, we can trust the honesty of others if we know them to love God and their fellow-man. It works both ways. Developing mutual trust is a worthy objective and a place to start to rebuild our loyalty to moral standards.

Neither the codes of conduct of corporations nor the laws and ordinances of government can restrain the leader who seeks to operate no higher than the minimum standards, and these restraints on conduct certainly won't build character. It has always been the task of church to point leaders to the high road, to challenge their *moral sense*, and to teach them *moral wisdom* from the example of Christ.

Christian ethics places the burden on each person to *love their neighbor enough to make laws unnecessary*. This sounds idealistic but it is not different from Socrates' search for what makes a worthwhile life, although it is an expansion. He recognized that the search for moral wisdom is closely associated with one's treatment of others. Even though most of the specific standards of conduct come from the historic study of ethics from the Greek philosophers, they did not have the perfect example to demonstrate their philosophy. We do have an example in Christ. *Christian ethics is the personal pursuit of a worthwhile life through moral wisdom learned from the example and teachings of Jesus Christ.* This makes it different from ethics tied closely to the law of the land.

Recall the characteristics of Christian ethics listed in Appendix B to Chapter I:

1.   It is what guides the lives of Christians

2.   It is not driven by laws, codes, or conventions but it acknowledges the need for agreed upon normative standards of conduct.

3.   It depends upon individual love for one's fellowman and on commitment to constant search for a worthwhile life.

4.   It is a revealed ethic from the model exemplified and taught by Christ

◆   ◆   ◆

I can't seem to avoid these philosophical and theological notions. But, as I think about it, none of us should. We are not talking about making widgets. I've gone through this philosophical and theological explanation of Christian ethics because it is essential to understanding what has gone wrong in our Christian systemized society. Complexities of the pervasive systems I have been talking about call for even greater effort from the church to make men and women good.

10

IT'S A COMPLEX WEB

It is time to sum up. Even though most studies do indicate rising crime rates, growing lack of concern for moral standards, and disdain for ethical expectations, it has not been my purpose to re-hash these issues directly. Rather, my purpose has been to focus on the enabling environment of our systems and organized society and the unique need in these arenas for strong leadership. All objective studies using traditional standards tell us that there has been a significant abrogation of our moral standards. True, some of the increase is nothing more than better reporting by the media and better records by police, the census bureau, and others. Nevertheless, even factoring this in, there is much evidence of the mischief in business, government, education, the professions, and even the church.

It's not that we should ignore the motivations of dishonest, decadent, or immoral people, but there is also a duty of the leaders of our systems of society to mitigate the motivations to do wrong. Specifically, the people I am concerned about are those good leaders who fail to recognize the special moral responsibility of their positions and, consequently, they fall back on what I have called *passive self-interest.*

I am talking about leaders at all levels of our great systems who have allowed our American culture to *normalize its own moral sickness.* In the Preface, I identified the systems of society that are of concern.

* Our government influenced economy that nurtures "spend now/pay later" economic decisions,

* The corporate form of business organization that separates management from ownership,

* Education of professional managers that went too long ignoring their ethical responsibilities,

* Gradual acceptance of little ethical indiscretions that do not interfere with a larger objective of profits, business plans, etc., and

* The waning influence of the church, particularly its failure to speak out on the misconduct that ultimately grows into front-page misconduct.

LET'S PULL IT TOGETHER

Let me summarize the issues that have contributed to good people accepting moral sickness:

1. We have normalized our own moral sicknesses because leaders of our great institutions have not put early intervention systems high on their agenda, before subordinates have become addicted to decadence and the immorality in their surroundings.

2. We have failed to teach young people moral lessons as they progress through school at all levels from grammar school to colleges and universities.

3. The shift from a market-driven economy to one heavily influenced by government taxation and expenditures has created *wealth without work*, an attitude of entitlements that replaced a work ethic, and an *enabling environment* that functions as an incubator for a mischief. Let's be clear though. Economic systems do not cause immorality, people do.

4. The corporation that insulates business leaders from society's ethical (and legal) expectations has been abused by executives who are shielded from accountability by the corporate shell that is supposed to stimulate economic growth for everyone. In other words, the corporation itself has also created an *enabling environment* for devious people who want to abuse it or even morally responsible leaders who take the path of least resistance.

5. The corporate shield has been a factor, but the new breed, the professional manager, whose focus is on growth, ROI, market share, profit targets, business plans, and the boss's demands has also failed us too often because of the enormous pressure on managers to perform. The opportunities for financial gain frequently have been too great for some managers in the absence of moral and ethical education that could empower them to handle their awesome duties. There are also some good people who occasionally do bad things along with the usual suspects who have a natural propensity to mischief. Both, with too much power, have provided fuel to the decadence that is burning in the industrialized world.

6. The law has proven inadequate in motivating the "high road" needed to reduce the scandalous behavior of executives, political leaders, athletes, entertainers, and too many others. But, then, it isn't supposed to do this. The law is only supposed to maintain order, not make us good.

7. In addition to the massive criminal infractions reported to us within organizations of all types, they are only the tip of the iceberg. *Big oaks from little acorns grow.* Thus, it is important that we concentrate on the first-time unethical issue as a preventive measure. Whistle blowing has nasty connotations that no one likes so we learn to accept little infractions. But if we can transform the image of whistle blowers into neighbors who feel good about helping neighbors, it can only help.

8. We have also suffered by the lack of a strong commitment to the economic rules of competition, which has been given minimum attention by too many business executives and government officials. Competition simply to satisfy excessive pride can engender unethical or, at least, distasteful, responses. Rather competition should be to provide better products and services to the most people at the lowest prices and thereby to generate energy for economic growth—always within the rules of the game.

9. Then, the church has lost its impact in the world of leaders. In truth, the concept of "one church" doesn't exist in the minds of many people today. We are completely divided with little interest in how to re-unite behind Christ's mission for his church. Each denomination has its own internal troubles. They are over-matched with the bigness of business and the government. Most serious, the larger churches and denominations have been timid in teaching the basic concept of *moral wisdom* that Christian executives must have to remain free to seek God's will individually and personally.

10. In total, we now have highly organized systems that nurture each other and make no demand on our moral sense.

FORGING THE LINK BETWEEN ECONOMICS AND FAITH

The irony of our condition is that our predecessors created both economic and governance systems assuming that there would always be a strong moral influence among us—the church. One more time, when Adam Smith described a supply and demand economic system, he was speaking as a moral philosopher (preacher) in the Anglican Church of Scotland and England, a professor of moral philosophy, and an astute observer of the social order in Britain. Smith, not yet an economist, was not trying to launch a new self-interested economic system, enlightened though it may be. He was simply describing a social system based upon his faith in the goodness of most people. He wasn't anymore naive than Jefferson with his belief in the individual moral sense. When you think about it, isn't this the same thing as the expectations of Christ and his teachings: to develop relationships with one another based upon the innate goodness, the moral wisdom, of Christians.

Smith, Jefferson, and all of the shapers of our country assumed that there would always be a church influencing the economic, political and social affairs of the people. I'm not as sure they envisioned the explosion of denominations within the church.

As Chapter IV pointed out, the shift to Keynesian economics in the 1930's did as it was intended. It lifted us out of the depths of the Great Depression. We only listened to part of Keynes's message, and ignored the parts that called for fiscal responsibility; spend less money than tax receipts to reduce inflation and deficits. We have since learned the error of such a policy, but, even so, it clearly illustrated the need for major programs on which to spend tax funds. There's the rub. From that point, it has been open season for political demagogues to argue for their "fair share" of the pie, to make promises to gullible voters, to conjure up "pork barrel legislation," and, in the process, create "wealth without work."

Unfortunately, we now hear of some local churches falling victim to Keynes's enticing message. We hear more and more about the need to steer government funds through churches to deal with poverty, child care, and other social problems. The "informed buyer/informed seller" equation is under more pressure today than ever because we have normalized appeals to government to fund the work of the church. Sure, the economy has grown and people have become wealthier, but opportunities for wealth without work have challenged the ethics of transactions for too many people, probably all of us. So now we want government to fund church programs.

It has been said many times that government funds, like drugs, become habit-forming—an entitlement. More than that, it becomes a sedative to relieve one's personal sense of duty to help the poor, etc. Government entitlement dupes us into thinking we are eliminating poverty, creating jobs, reducing crime, fighting teen-age pregnancy, and other social problems. History and analysis of our society tells us otherwise. The stark reality is that for every human helped by government social spending, two others are placed in some kind of depraved condition. Government programs do not offer the opportunity to change lives, only to care for immediate needs.

While Jefferson's ideas prevailed in the formative years of our country, it can easily be argued that we have yet to prove him right. Can we trust ourselves to govern ourselves? Can we trust ourselves to resist unrestrained self-interest? The answer hinges upon whether one feels we still have the collective moral wisdom to handle the job. This moral condition depends upon each of us exercising moral wisdom developed by commitment to instruction in the family with strong church support. If we have any remote claim to being a Christian nation, this is its basis.

This raises the crucial role for the nation's moral agent, the church. There is a strong opinion among people with fundamentalist attitudes about the church, characterized by such men as Jerry Falwell, that the United States has a special role in the expansion of Christianity. They believe that the United States is indeed called by God for a special purpose, even to be Israel's successor. There is no question that we have been specially blessed with enormous resources, and this puts a great moral responsibility on us. But the responsibility is on each of us rather than on our loosely formed government. Our form of government, unique among all others, is intended to leave morality, ethics, and matters of faith with the people, individually and personally, nurtured by a strong church. That's the way our forefathers wanted it, and the way we inherited it. It was never intended that we turn over our moral obligations to government.

The awareness of Christian ethics based upon individual moral wisdom is evident in both our supply and demand economic system and our democratic system of government. It seems illogical that we can function with these broad freedoms unless we are at least willing to attempt to live by Christ's example and teachings. Systems based upon a strong moral undergirding of a particular faith eventually will fail when people discover that the undergirding is not there. Remember the Basuto proverb: *If a man does away with his traditional way of living and throws away his good customs, he had better first make certain that he has something of value to replace them.* The philosophical and religious glue from our founding fathers has begun to rot away.

Some argue that the expectations of our founding fathers are no longer relevant, that our high-flying complex society is too far removed from the guiding principles of 1787. We are certainly more diverse, but if the principles are to be changed, we need to update them by the will of people committed to the faith. It is heartening in these early days of this century to hear so much more concern for faith issues and for the need to speak out. The Silent Majority of the 1980's eventually lost their impetus, but I have to believe that there is a majority of Americans with moral backbone who want to be heard, who want their leaders to be men and women of faith. Maybe a revisit to our heritage would allow this to happen.

We are often disillusioned by our leaders and we become discouraged with our systems. We are creatures of choice more than all other creatures. Some people, like Osama Bin Laden, Saddam Hussein, or Adolph Hitler chose to make evil sadistic choices. Does this mean God was wrong in giving us so much choice? No, although I most confess that sometimes it is hard to understand why the freedom to choose is so universal. Nevertheless, I will stick to my premise that there was a point where someone might have changed the direction of their lives, even of these aberrations to humanity.

I am convinced that in each case, there were times when good people with moral wisdom could have made a difference. For instance, as evil as Hitler was, he could not have achieved power without the degradation and poverty in Germany left by the Great Depression and by the allies' insistence upon reparations after WWI. In 1932, he seemed to be the person to bring back the dignity Germany once knew. How wrong they were. The depraved psychology in Germany was just the cesspool Hitler needed. What if someone of importance, a leader, had taken a personal interest in him after his WWI experience? Maybe the world would not have had to endure WWII.

Each of these three maniacs seem to defy my notion that frequently we can prevent leaders from harming themselves and others, if we could intervene in their lives early with strong doses of moral wisdom. Nevertheless, they are atypical and classic examples of my "1% group," the pathological wrongdoers. Okay, but I still believe that early in their lives there was an opportunity. In such situations, God has raised up strong moral individuals to oppose them. Maybe, this is why Jesus said, "There will always be wars and threats of wars." He knew we would not always be able to change lives.

However, as serious as world conflict is, we are told by the experts that it is too serious to be left to the teachings of any religion. We may not be able to see all things down the road, but we are charged to keep trying to change the lives of people, even those bent on mayhem. However, it's the everyday normal challenges to normal people that can be addressed by a strong church carrying out its mission of developing moral wisdom. It's a place to start. And this is my hope and prayer.

Moral degeneration is like the well-publicized snowball that picks up mass and velocity as it rolls down the mountain. The time to stop its destruction is at the top of the mountain.

FROM PHILOSOPHY TO PRACTICALITY

I have a cross-stitched picture in my office, made by my wife, which reads, "Lord, save us from the gnats; we can handle the elephants ourselves." It's cute, and perhaps there was a day when it was reasonably appropriate, but not today. We are becoming less able to handle the gnats and, consequently, less experienced to deal with the unethical elephants. If you are one of those leaders who understands how little indiscretions grow into big ones, you are on the right path to leading a moral organization. You know how important early intervention is to preventing ethical infractions (avoiding the gnats).

But what is unethical? Even though it has not been my intent to talk directly about forms of good and bad conduct, it may be helpful to recognize it when we see it. We have discussed the need for ethical conduct, but how do we know unethical conduct down in the trenches when we see it? What does an unethical act look like? Kenneth Blanchard and Norman Vincent Peale gave us two means of identifying them in their book, *The Power of Ethical Management*, 1988. The first approach was their "Five P's":

Purpose—Will my decision or action compromise (cheat) the purpose of my company (organization), family, faith, or my own life?

Pride—When my decision or action (deceit) is complete, will I be proud to tell others what I have done? Am I taking action only to satisfy my own self-interest?

Patience—Am I taking action or making this decision because I don't have the patience to wait for a better (honest) alternative?

Persistence—Can I "stick to my guns" even in face of opposition from colleagues, superiors, friends, family, or fellow church members (resist the crowd)?

Perspective—(Be careful with this one.) Do I get perspective (moral guidance) in my decisions from my actions in the past, from what I see others doing, from what others want me to do, or from God's expectations for me?

Perspective is achieved through the daily exercise of one's moral sense. It's not only what others think, although this is important; it may not even be achieved by what you might think yourself (but don't ignore your own attitude). It must also brings into the picture God's wisdom, which we get through prayer, meditation, and Bible reading. It's the search for Jesus' example and teachings, and what I have called *moral wisdom.*

With this kind of perspective, the other P's will become easier; *purpose, pride, patience, and persistence.* Certainly, it provides a base from which to assess other ethical considerations.

Blanchard and Peale also provided us with three more practical, on the spot, ethical check questions one can use when in doubt;

1.   Is it legal? Will I be violating either civil or criminal law, company code of conduct, honor code, or organizational policy? (This is just a starting point.)

2.   Is it balanced? Is it fair to all concerned in the short-term as well as the long-term? Did each participant in the transaction have full information? Does it promote a win/win relationship?

3.   How will it make me feel about myself? Will it make me proud? Would I feel good if my decision were published in the newspaper? Would I feel good if my family knew about it?

We are each a bundle of choices walking around ready to be exercised. If the exercise of my choices restricts someone else from making theirs, without their permission, it is more than likely unethical. Before making my choice, it may be helpful to walk through one of the above sets of analytical questions. I need to wear other's shoes before I act.

I have been pressing the point rather hard that *every society normalizes its own sickness.* As you think about it, by this time you might agree and have thought of examples you know about. If you don't agree, it is all the more important that I amplify this concept. What makes this adage more apparent for me are leader's "do nothing" *passive self-interests.* If we do nothing about small ethical infractions, we normalize our sickness. Let me revisit these passive self-interests again (as Yogi Berra might say).

* Everybody else does it, so why should I try to stop it.

* We've always done it. I don't think it does any harm.

* I'm not the conscience of the company. It's not my job to blow the whistle.

* Don't break the law (or the code of ethics), but get the job done.

* I can't tell someone else what is right or wrong for him or her.

I have been suggesting some approaches to regain our moral fiber, but let me summarize them because I believe they are imperative to rebuilding our moral backbone:

1. The Christian church needs to teach what it believes, really believes, without apologizing to its detractors within the faith and without.

2. We can put greater emphasis upon church education to train (educate) Christians. What do we believe and how does it apply to the workweek?

3. Families cannot handle the moral training of children alone because the concept of the family, itself, is rapidly eroding. The church needs to reinforce them with sound instruction for parents as well as children about the Christian Ethic.

4. Secular schools, public as well as private, cannot completely educate their students without including moral education and, in the United States, this means Christian education.

5. In the workplace, everyone should be able to see moral wisdom at work. Leaders should demonstrate a good life as Socrates sought and as Jesus exemplified.

RECONNECTING WORK WITH FAITH

There is really nothing new in the above list. The major point is that we need to bring the church into the process of defining morality and ethical conduct. Companies can benefit from demonstrating that they know the connection between work and faith, as can be seen from some ideas that have already helped in a few companies include:

- Periodic Prayer, meditation, and Bible study.

- A moral ombudsman with whom people will feel comfortable talking about moral matters in their work (perhaps from outside the company.

- Ethics audits to assess the way lower echelon executives are exercising their ethical duty. In larger companies, this auditor probably should report to the Board of Director's Audit Committee. The goal here is not so much to find wrongdoers, as it is to ferret out *passive self-interest* among managers, re-educate the negligent ones, and encourage ethical decisions and action.

- Certainly, ethics statements need periodic review, they must be discussed in seminars, and need to be practiced by the leaders.

- The euphemistic concept of "whistle blowers" can and should be replaced with "neighbors helping neighbors stay out of trouble." The moral ombudsman can play a major part in this effort. In Matthew 18: 15-18, Christians are given a process for reconciling differences. First, the observer of another's wrongdoing could speak privately with the offender. If necessary to go farther, a third person could be invited to participate as a quiet objective voice. If all else fails, the matter probably cannot easily be taken to the church as a whole (not the courts), but possibly to some form of committee of respected employees who could counsel with authority. With some adaptation, this process could be helpful in creating an ethical environment in which all employees feel good about themselves and their employer.

The appropriateness of this process for Christians is recorded in the Epistle of James, that short, pragmatic, and direct book of instruction for new Christians. It acknowledges our responsibility for our neighbors;

> *…if any one among you wanders from the truth and some one brings him back, let him know that whoever brings back a sinner (wrong-doer) from the error of his ways will save his soul from death and will cover (avoid) a multitude of sins (infractions).* James 5: 19-20)

The task of connecting work and faith in government is daunting, but still possible. Years ago, one of our most prominent political figures had just won his first election to Congress. He told me that he had a long agenda of things he believed to be needed in the country and which he felt was within his Christian understanding of "the right thing to do." Nevertheless, he also felt that he could not be re-elected by pushing legislation that would never get through Congress. He was right and wrong. He was part of a *system* that requires legislators to satisfy an electorate. If that electorate has lost its moral undergirding, then the congressman was right. Two decades later, he was still in office and his agenda was still on the shelf, drawing dust.

Saying that, I am looking at the issue much as churches have looked at immoral conduct in corporations. I am over-awed by our massive government, and not looking at the individual government executives and legislators. The institution is enormous and out of control, but it is still within the grasp of normal, moral human beings. Thus, it is still possible that early intervention in the lives of government leaders before they become leaders can perhaps provide a long-term solution. It's a dream, but we haven't had much success with pragmatism.

We do still have a democratic process that gives people the greatest opportunity to participate in government. On the other hand, we have also created a "candy store" for self-serving, smooth-talking scoundrels to rob our nation of its financial and moral strength. Somehow, we have to replace self-interested politicians with service-minded statesmen who truly are there to represent the people. How naïve can I get? I've already said more laws will not help. Perhaps, bringing our Christian heritage into the 21st Century might do it.

I am neither naïve nor arrogant enough to assume any one person can solve the enormous problems we have in our government. None of these ideas, or any others, have much chance of making an impact, without a strong church teaching moral wisdom to guide our moral sense. When you think about it, our legal system, based upon precedence, means it is experiences of the people that ultimately make the law. This is far different from the statutory systems: the Roman legal system, Judaic law, and Islamic law. In these systems morality flows from the law, just the opposite from our law of precedence. Even if this is a little idealistic today, it does make the point that the people who establish the precedence need moral training.

If this is so, then it is imperative that the church pick up its responsibility for moral training, for the development of *moral wisdom*, to prepare political leaders for their awesome political and economic responsibility. Someone is sure to point out that the church does this.

The church does indeed address the spiritual needs of its followers through worship, mission work, charity, fellowship, and Christian education. Nevertheless, the church is not resisting the pressure from other institutions and systems who tell Christians to keep its doctrine to itself. Consequently, our charge to take the faith to the world is not getting enough emphasis. Part of this problem comes from lack of understanding of the Christian faith. If development of moral wisdom is the church's task and purpose, then we need to develop people. And that means education!

Christians, today, don't know what they should believe about issues like:

- homosexual conduct,

- extra-marital sex,

- marriage and divorce,

- abuse of power,

- ethics of competing,

- deceptive advertising (lying),

- qualifications of ministers,

- attitudes about other faiths,

- racial harmony,

- foreign policy anchored by military strength,

- economic policy regarding wealth and the income gap,

- the effect of parent's self-interest on children,

- and a host of other social issues today.

It's about education, folks; faith-based education. If the church intends to educate us on these difficult topics, it seems good that there be a clearly defined church position. The church, or even the separate denominations thereof, needs to decide what its position is, what Christ said to us, and then project its position to the world for better or worse. If we are going to lose members and money, let's do it for the right reasons, not because the "mamby-pamby" message is weak. The religious web that we weave today is complex.

We have often heard the "carrot or the stick" story about how to motivate a mule. Somehow, this analogy is supposed to say something about motivating people. It does, if we apply a little imagination. In recent years, we have evolved into a "carrot" society, meaning we rely on feel good, positive relationships to get the best out of followers. In many businesses, it is the attitude inherent in their motivational efforts, and maybe it has helped improve productivity and quality, but "carrot" relationships have not stopped the rise in unethical and illegal conduct. Perhaps, it wasn't intended to do this. The "carrot" society is probably a direct reaction to the "stick" motivators of the scientific management practices of the early 20th Century, which didn't make us moral either.

However, we can interpolate this homespun wisdom into our search for morality. We need both the carrot and the stick, as we always have. If we consider the law to be the "stick", we know the law alone will not make us moral, but it cannot maintain order if we are personally pre-disposed to mischief. The law can and does provide needed punitive motivators to maintain order, that are regrettably necessary. However, if we depend only on the law, codes, rules, or consensus opinions, we have done nothing to attract the mule to walk the high road. We also need the "carrot." If we do not give people a "carrot," meaning the example and teachings of Christ, they will find rightness/wrongness solely by seeking the lowest common denominator from the law or from the social standards of close friends and associates.

In our society, isn't it the work of the church to replace founding values with "something of value?" Yet, instead of looking to the church, we have been left to look for new laws, codes, conventions, and social correctness that only treat external symptoms of moral sickness. The cure comes from treating causes of the disease after the proper diagnosis, the example and teachings of Christ.

Let's not get things out of perspective. The church is not dead. Its roots are deep in our heritage and, more importantly, it is God's instrument for expanding the faith. The issue is with those who want to limit the church to a Sunday morning feel good experience. This is not all bad and it may look good in the short-run, but eventually God's total plan for salvation must be carried out, even when it hurts.

In seminars, I leave participants with a small card that reads: *My soul is at work with me today.* Its purpose is to remind them that they each have the ability and obligation to make their own moral judgments. It is intended as reinforcement in an environment in which independent moral judgments are often taboo. Interestingly, I have been asked after every seminar to send more cards. Why is this simple idea received so well? Perhaps it's because people are hungry for moral support, for moral leadership, and for moral encouragement. I think Jesus knew this when he challenged his disciples to go to the world preaching and teaching *moral wisdom,—love one another.*

0-595-32527-0

Printed in the United States
23210LVS00008B/70-87